W9-BXY-280

SHINING

Ole Smoky Moonshine Family Cookbook

JESSI BAKER

Photography by Angie Mosier

Andrews McMeel
PUBLISHING®

This book is dedicated to two of my favorite people: my grandmother, the first person I knew to make her own bone broth, taught me that kindness matters, manners are extremely important, and hard work defines your character; and my husband, Joe, without whom this book wouldn't have happened, and whose friendship back in our tender high school years shaped my life.

SHINING

Ole Smoky Moonshine
Family Cookbook

CONTENTS

ACKNOWLEDGMENTS

I'm very thankful for the opportunity to write this book. I love food and I love cooking, and to be able to combine those interests with our moonshine business is a blessing.

First and foremost, I'd like to thank my husband for being the ultimate taste tester and for providing endless encouragement and critiques. To my kiddos, you're my everything, and I love inventing recipes that make your stomachs full and your hearts happy. To everyone in the Ole Smoky family, thanks for your diligence and hard work continuing the growth and development of such a special product and brand. And to Cory and Tony, thanks for your partnership in creating this business. To my brother, Chuck, thank you for keeping it all together.

Finally, to those women, some sisters by blood and others just loyal friends, who lifted me up and encouraged me to believe in myself and my food, I love you: Bev and Jill, who helped me chop and test recipes; Sarah and Maggie, for being interested and giving me good feedback from the very beginning; Kristen, for formatting and everything in between; Abi, for being the ultimate, detail-oriented, last-minute editor; and Tiff and Stormie, for being the best second hands there could ever be.

Lastly, music is food for the soul. I hope you enjoy the excerpts from songs, either about Tennessee or about moonshining, headlining each chapter.

CHAPTER ONE

HISTORY OF MOONSHINING IN APPALACHIA

You hardly ever saw Grandaddy down here
He only come to town about twice a year
He'd buy a hundred pounds of yeast and some copper line
Everybody knew that he made moonshine
Now the revenue man wanted Grandaddy bad
He headed up the holler with everything he had
'Fore my time but I've been told
He never come back from Copperhead Road

Copperhead Road by Steve Earle

The roots of moonshine can be traced back to our Scots-Irish ancestors who first settled here in the Smoky Mountains during the latter half of the 1700s. The craft of distilling spirits evolved from generations of making whiskey in Ireland and Scotland, so it made sense for those traditions to continue when the settlers migrated here to the mountains of Appalachia.

The rugged ways of mountain life forced these pioneers to become a tough and fiercely independent group of people. Over the years, the federal government established numerous taxes and laws regulating the manufacturing of spirits. These changes in laws created an environment for those in the shadows of the mountains to skirt enforcement and maintain a competitive advantage through the illicit trade of moonshine.

After losing revenue to the underground network of liquor trade, the Revenue Bureau of the Treasury Department transformed their "collectors" into a policing authority.

This enforcement of revenue collection marked the beginning of the cat-and-mouse wars of the moonshiners and revenuers.

The temperance movement led to Prohibition in 1920. Prohibition banned the manufacture, sale, and consumption of alcohol. The demand for moonshine skyrocketed—especially in the big cities where organized crime drove strong demand for a dependable supply of liquor.

The moonshiners needed to keep up with demand, so they adjusted their recipes and formulas accordingly. The distillers would do whatever it took to keep their supply chain flowing, but they faced many challenges. The mountains are full of stories of young men who ran liquor. The tough business of making spirits in the backwoods of the mountains led to numerous clashes between moonshiners and government agents.

Throughout much of our nation's early history, the people of the mountains chose to avoid the conflicts that embroiled our nation. Outsiders were not trusted, and the clannish ways of the mountain people insulated them from much of the outside world.

As government developed laws to regulate or restrict the making of spirits, our

The Newport Plain Talk, Newport, Tennessee

BIG BUSINESS -- A still with a capacity of 300 gallons or six barrels was confiscated by Jefferson County Sheriff's Department officials about 6 a.m. Monday northeast of the Chestnut Hill section of the county. Sheriff Elmer Franklin said he had known a still was in the area for some time but had been unable to locate it. He received the information during the weekend on its location. The sheriff said the still had been operated within the past 10 days to two weeks. While the worm and cap could not be found, the deputies confiscated the cooling tank and pot. From left are Deputy Sheriffs George Eslinger, Paul Knight, John Holt and Leonard Huff, Sheriff Franklin, and Deputies Gordon Taylor and Charles Woods. (Photo Courtesy Morristown Citizen - Tribune.)

ancestors took exception to these outsiders getting involved in their affairs. Mountain folk have always had a healthy mistrust of government. This way of life is memorialized in one of Tennessee's state songs: "Once two strangers climbed Ole Rocky Top looking for a moonshine still. Strangers ain't come down from Rocky Top. Reckon they never will."

When prohibition was repealed in 1933, the market for moonshine grew thin, but even through the 1950s, moonshining continued in the mountains and hills of Appalachia. Over the years, thousands of stills were destroyed by federal agents. Moonshine continued to be a problem for federal authorities into the 1960s and '70s, but very few illegal alcohol cases are heard in the courts today.

Stills Seized In County Tuesday

Two young Cocke County men were arrested on Tuesday and charged with violation of Internal Revenue Law. They were identified as R. L. Shelton, 19 and Darrell Shelton, 18, brothers, Route 3, Del Rio.

A raid was conducted at 9 a.m. in the Round Mountain Section of Cocke County when two stills were seized, a 520 gallon capacity and the other 310 gallon capacity and a total of 800 gallons of mash, according to Gray Cline, special investigator in charge, Tobacco and Fire Arms Division, U. S. Treasury Dept. The raid was conducted by the Tobacco and Fire Arms Division and Tennessee State ABC Agents.

The two were taken before Commissioner James McSween Jr. where hearing was waived and they were released under $1,000 bond each for appearance in Federal Court.

Any person or persons having information on distilleries or liquor movements please contact Mr. Cline, at P. O. Box 336, Greeneville, or phone 638-4281 collect. All information is strictly confidential, Mr. Cline said. Rewards will be paid for information leading to the arrest or seizure of any distillery.

Large Distillery Seized; Newport Man Arrested

The largest distillery in months was seized in the Bogard section of Cocke County on Thursday, Feb. 4, at 1:15 p.m. according to Special Investigator Ray Cline.

This distillery consisted of six 520 gallon galvanized stills, 2,000 gallons of mash, and a quantity of jugs and other distilling equipment. A 1957 Pontiac was also seized at the distillery, Cline said.

Sherman Leroy Hudson, 1104 Woodlawn Ave., Newport, was arrested at the distillery site, according to Cline. Other arrest are expected to follow, according to Cline.

Hudson was taken before United States Magistrate James C. McSween, Newport, where a hearing was set for February 26. Hudson was released after posting a $1,000 bond pending federal Court.

Ray Cline, special investigator in charge of Alcohol, Tobacco, and Firearm Division, ask anyone having information on illegal distilleries to contact him at P. O. Box 336, Greeneville, Tennessee or call 638-4281, collect.

Cocke County Deputy Arrested For Operating Unregistered Still

Federal and state ABC agents seized an unregistered distillery from the residence of Crawford Junior Holt, age 53, Route 3, Newport.

Agent Ray Cline, ATU Unit head for the ten-county area including Cocke and adjoining counties said, "Holt identified himself as a bonded deputy sheriff and said he had served for the past 15 years as a deputy in Cocke County. Agent Cline said, "Holt had in his possession, his bond, deputy badge, gun and blackjack."

The County Court Clerk's office said they did not have a bond recorded for Holt.

A check with the Register of Deeds office revealed Holt's bond failed to be registered, however, Mrs. Haynes called the next day saying she had found Holt's bond. A short time later J. L. Moore, Cocke County Tax Assessor called and asked if the newspaper had asked Mrs. Haynes about Holt's bond. Mr. Moore said that Holt was not a bonded deputy. A few minutes later Mrs. Haynes called back and said she was wrong, that Holt had registered a bond in 1966 and it expired in 1968. Another county officer said he thought Holt's bond had been revoked weeks ago.

Sheriff Tom O'Dell told the PORT PLAIN TALK ... ning that Holt is ... d had not been a ... is term and part ...

... till was seized F ... 7 at 12:05 p.m. ... 520-gallon po ... 320-gallon po ... gallons mash.

The still had a daily production capacity of 44 gallons and if the distillery were allowed to continue to operate, it would cost the government $462 dollars per day in Federal taxes.

Holt was arraigned before U.S. Commissioner James C. McSween of Newport, Holt was released on his own recognizance.

Officers said Holt was arrested sometime ago but was released on a technicality.

Anyone having any information about unregistered distilleries in Cocke County are asked to contact Ray Cline, Special Investigator in charge, P.O. Box 336, Greeneville or call collect 638-4281. All information is confidential.

Whitson Announces For Court Clerk Of Cocke County

Still Raided At Hall's Top

Federal and State agents raided an unregistered still at 6:30 a.m. March 7, at Hall's Top in Cocke County.

Two 500 gallon pot-type stills were seized along with 1,000 gallons mash and other miscellaneous distilling equipment.

Arrested were Thomas Ray Webb, Route 3 Cosby, and George Phillips, Route 3 Cosby.

The men were taken before U.S. Commissioner James C. McSween and released under $1000 bond each.

Any information on distilleries operating in Cocke County will be appreciated. Anyone having such information is urged to call or write the Alcohol Tax Unit in Greeneville, or write Ray Cline, Special Investigator in Charge, P.O. Box 336 Greeneville, Tennessee or Alcohol and Tax Unit, U.S. Treasury Department.

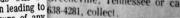

SHERIFF NETS BIG HAUL

EAST TENNESSEE RYE—Fifty-five gallons of it and more in the makin'. That's what Sheriff J. Wesley Brewer and his men found in a house a quarter-of-a-mile off Middlebrook pike in the Eighth district early Wednesday afternoon.

Rye mash in 18 50-gallon barrels "was just a-working when we got there," said one of the officers. The operators were making a run at the time.

The above picture shows Sheriff Brewer (right), the rye in half-gallon jars, the neat and nifty 60-gallon copper still, and one of the operators, Jackson Watson, Vestal, in overalls.

The complete distilling outfit was found in the attic of the house. to the left of Watson may be seen a lookout window.

Watson and Brownlow Underwood, also of Vestal, were at the still when the officers arrived. They are now out on bond on charges of manufacturing liquor.

Officers making the raid were Sheriff Brewer and Deputies Bill Brewer, Lonas, Loveday, Reed, and Craig.

RUBBING ALCOHOL is mixed with the moonshine to give it ... appearance of being stronger.

Today, the tried-and-true traditions of those early mountain settlers live on in Ole Smoky Tennessee Moonshine. Making moonshine is a craft in which we take a lot of pride. Staying true to our roots, we incorporate the recipes and traditions that have been passed down through generations of families in the Virginias, Carolinas, Kentucky, Georgia, and Tennessee. Our ancestors were growing corn and making whiskey here before Tennessee was a state, and after years of having to hide from the law, we're proud to finally be able to legally share the best spirits in the mountains.

CHAPTER TWO

MY FAMILY AND OLE SMOKY MOONSHINE

Smoky Mountain memories
About my home in Tennessee
Yesterday keeps calling me,
Calling me home
Mountains rising in my soul
Higher than the dreams I've known
Misty eyed, they cling to me, my Smoky Mountain memories

Smoky Mountain Memories performed by Larry Sparks

never thought I'd be a moonshiner. I grew up in Gatlinburg, Tennessee, a small mountain community that serves as the gateway to Great Smoky Mountains National Park. My mom's parents moved to the mountains from Philadelphia, Pennsylvania, in the late 1940s. They made candy for a living. My dad, born in Brooklyn and raised in Long Island, New York, became a local judge in Tennessee. My mother was a stay-at-home mom who raised six children. I completed a science project on distilling alcohol when I was in the sixth grade, and I remember seeing my first real moonshine still somewhere around that time.

My grandparents started Ole Smoky Candy Kitchen in Gatlinburg in 1950. Every day after school I walked to the candy kitchen to work for my grandmother. I packed taffy, ran errands, and learned about Gatlinburg business and its relevance as a tourist destination. As the oldest child in my family, I always dreamed of running the candy kitchen one day. As I grew up, though, fate led me down a different path.

I went to Georgetown University for college, studied Spanish and Art History, and then came home to Tennessee for law school. I married my high school sweetheart, Joe Baker, a lawyer, whose family enjoys a long, colorful history of living in the Smoky Mountains.

Joe and I spent our first years of marriage working hard as prosecutors in the district attorney's office. When I became pregnant with our second child, I was fortunate to be able to step away from the practice of law and focus on caring for our growing family. Joe transitioned from working for the government to building a busy, private law practice that increasingly soaked up his time, and if I'm being completely honest, his soul, too. At home, we enjoyed the benefits of a pretty comfortable and stable existence for several years, but I could tell that he was becoming increasingly agitated and ready for a change.

In 2009, when the Tennessee legislature passed a bill that legalized distilling spirits, Joe quickly decided to make moonshine. I'll never forget the morning he came into the room where I was nursing our youngest baby and told me that he was starting a distillery. Moonshine? We had three young children, two mortgages, and a busy law practice. I couldn't

help but wonder how this was going to work. Although he'd been raised around moonshine and comes from a long line (over two hundred years-worth) of Eastern Tennessee moonshiners, we were both very much yuppies living in an upscale Knoxville, Tennessee, neighborhood.

But like any good, stubborn hillbilly would do, Joe persisted. He believed that he was on the verge of something special, and with the help of partners Cory Cottingim and Tony Breeden, he never looked back. In less than nine months from our first conversation, Ole Smoky Moonshine was open for business.

Through our family, the company's roots can be traced back to the early settlers of the Smoky Mountains. In 2009, the law changed and suddenly, it was legal to make, distill, and sell the infamous bootlegger's hooch. It was at that point that we decided to bring our artistry of superior moonshine-making to the world at large. In the earliest days of the business, our kitchen was the laboratory from which flavors such as Apple Pie, Blackberry, Sweet Tea, and Lemon Drop Moonshine were born.

And the world welcomed it. Ole Smoky is the leading distiller of premium moonshine in the United States and the first federally licensed distillery in the history of East Tennessee. Our lines of moonshine and whiskey are now sold in all fifty states and in fifty-four countries around the world. The business originated at our Gatlinburg distillery, "The Holler," where visitors can see and experience how Ole Smoky moonshine is made. Since its opening in 2010, Ole Smoky has expanded with three more locations, including "The Barn" in 2013 and "The Barrelhouse" in 2015, which produces the company's new whiskey line

that launched nationally in the fall of 2017. This year, 2019, marks the opening of the company's fourth distillery in Tennessee, this time in Nashville.

After several short but very hard and trying years, Ole Smoky Moonshine has grown into the most visited distillery in the world. We welcome over four million visitors from all over the world each year. Ole Smoky now retails globally and offers many creative flavors crafted from authentic family recipes. And while OIe Smoky has long been enjoyed on the porch from the jar, Ole Smoky now finds its shine in handcrafted cocktails of the finest order in establishments across the United States, including at some of the biggest music and sporting venues in the country.

Food is my language of love. I spend so much time in the kitchen that I wanted to write this book so that my children could have something tangible to go with the memories we've created together around food and our moonshine business. As a mom who loves to cook at home, I embrace the many ways moonshine can spice up everything from canning pickles and okra to making cupcakes and cobblers a little bit naughty. The recipes you'll find in this book are straightforward and easy to follow, but the results are exciting and delicious.

I've studied art and law in a classroom, but my education with food has been mostly self-propelled in my own kitchen. One year, because I expressed so much dedication to cooking, Joe gave me a week of boot camp at the Culinary Institute of America in Hyde Park. That was probably my favorite Christmas present I've ever received, and my family definitely reaped the rewards. I've certainly spent lots of time eating in restaurants, reading cookbooks, and enjoying food, but still, I'm not a chef; I'm a good cook who enjoys making simple, great-tasting food. The recipes in this book should reflect that, as well as the idea that you don't have to be a classically trained chef to make excellent food.

Not every recipe has moonshine in it. Though I guess you could add it to everything, I only added it where I believe it enhances the flavor. All the other recipes are things that we cook often at home, or things that are traditional and important to our family.

With this cookbook, I wanted to write something fresh, simple, and pure, just like the mountains we call home, and something similar to the original shine for which these mountains are famous. I had my hesitations in the early days, but now I'm proud to call myself a moonshiner, especially in the kitchen.

CHAPTER THREE
COCKTAILS

Once two strangers climbed ol' Rocky Top
Lookin' for a moonshine still
Strangers ain't come down from Rocky Top
Reckon they never will
Corn won't grow at all on Rocky Top
Dirt's too rocky by far
That's why all the folks on Rocky Top
Get their corn from a jar

Rocky Top by Felice and Boudleaux Bryant

BLACKBERRY LEMONADE

SERVES 1

This drink is like summer in a jar and celebrates the flavors of the season. A refreshing beverage that's a little bit sweet mixed with a little bit sour, it's the perfect cocktail for picnics or front porch sipping.

3 ounces Ole Smoky Blackberry Moonshine

3 ounces fresh lemonade

Ice

Fresh mint and lemon wheel, for garnish

Mix the moonshine and lemonade together and serve over ice in a mason jar. Garnish with fresh mint and a lemon wheel.

THE STUBBORN MULE

SERVES 1

My husband's hillbilly stubbornness is the inspiration behind the name of this drink. Try this version of the familiar Moscow Mule with Ole Smoky Original Corn Moonshine. I think you'll like it!

2 ounces Ole Smoky Original Corn Moonshine

4 ounces ginger beer

½ ounce freshly squeezed lime juice

Splash of bitters

Ice

Fresh mint and lime wedge, for garnish

Mix the moonshine, ginger beer, lime juice, and bitters together and serve over ice in a copper mug. Garnish with mint and a lime wedge.

SHINE NOG
SERVES 10

Every December, we host a Christmas cookie exchange. Kids and adults love this party because there is something for everyone, tons of cookies, a huge pot of steaming moonshine chili, and some holiday cocktails for the adults. Joe and I started making eggnog in our early twenties as a way of creating a family Christmas tradition. We did it the traditional way with eggs, cream, sugar, and bourbon, but as Ole Smoky grew and expanded its product line, we made a Shine Nog version of the eggnog that we'd been taking to parties for years. Here is a recipe that will always be a hit at a holiday party. It's meant for a crowd, so use a large bowl to mix the drink, and a soup ladle for serving.

2 (750-ml) jars Ole Smoky
    Shine Nog

1½ quarts vanilla ice cream

1 cup of your favorite bourbon

Cinnamon sticks, for serving

Mix all the ingredients together in a large punch bowl. Serve in small lowball glasses and garnish with cinnamon sticks.

BEER SHINEARITA
SERVES 4 TO 6

A beer shinearita is a great drink for the hottest of summer days, and it always disappears quickly when served. It's easy to make and even easier to drink. It's a great accompaniment to Ramps & Eggs (page 120) and Skillet-Fried Cornpones (page 47).

1 (12-ounce) can frozen limeade

1 cup Ole Smoky Original Corn Moonshine

½ cup Ole Smoky Margarita Moonshine

1 cup water

1 (12-ounce) beer (Use a lighter flavored beer, not too hoppy. I like a Yee-Haw Kolsch for this.)

Juice from 1 lime

Salt, for rimming glasses

Ice

1 lime cut into wedges, for garnish

Combine the limeade, moonshines, and water in a pitcher and stir well, until the frozen limeade has dissolved. Add the beer and lime juice, and stir again. If you prefer, salt the rims of mason jars and add ice to fill each glass. Pour the shinearita over the ice and serve immediately with lime wedges.

THE APPLE GINGER

SERVES 1

This is one of the original cocktail recipes created for Ole Smoky. What's not to love about Apple Pie Moonshine with a splash of citrus? I like this drink any time of year but especially enjoy sharing it in the fall.

2½ ounces Ole Smoky Apple Pie Moonshine

2½ ounces ginger ale

½ ounce freshly squeezed lime juice

Ice

2 Ole Smoky Moonshine Cherries, for garnish

Slice of lime, for garnish

Stir the moonshine, ginger ale, and lime juice together. Serve over ice in a small mason jar. Garnish with the cherries and a slice of lime.

SALTY CARAMEL SPIKED MILKSHAKE

SERVES 6

This could be a dessert, but I like it more as a festive cocktail for a winter party. It's especially tasty served in frosted lowball whiskey glasses rimmed with cinnamon and sugar.

Cinnamon and sugar, for rimming the glasses

1 cup Ole Smoky Salty Caramel Whiskey, plus extra for rimming the glasses

4 cups vanilla ice cream

1½ teaspoons pure vanilla extract

1 cup whole milk

6 pirouette cookies, for garnish

Mix the cinnamon and sugar together on a small plate. Using your finger, lightly wet the rim of each lowball glass with whiskey. Place the rim of each glass on the plate to coat with the cinnamon and sugar. Repeat with the other glasses, then put them all in the freezer to chill.

Combine 1 cup of whiskey, the ice cream, vanilla, and milk in a blender and blend until smooth. Serve in the frosted glasses and garnish with a pirouette cookie. It's incredibly tasty!

MOONSHINE MARY

SERVES 1

Bloody Marys and mimosas are staples for brunch when my family gets together, especially on New Year's Day. The moonshine adds a little kick to the basics.

3 ounces Ole Smoky White Lightnin' Moonshine

2 ounces tomato juice

1 teaspoon Worcestershire sauce

2 dashes of hot sauce

1 teaspoon horseradish

½ teaspoon freshly squeezed lemon juice

⅛ teaspoon freshly ground black pepper

Pinch of salt

Ice

Celery stick, olives, and lemon wedge, for garnish

You will need two highball glasses. Combine the moonshine, tomato juice, Worcestershire sauce, hot sauce, horseradish, lemon juice, pepper, and salt in one of the glasses. Stir well to combine. Add ice. Pour the mixture back and forth between the glasses until you are satisfied it's well combined, usually 3 or 4 times. Garnish with a celery stick, olives, and a lemon wedge, as you like.

APPALACHIAN SANGRIA
SERVES 8 TO 10

I spent my junior year of college in Madrid, Spain, and this drink is my way of connecting two cultures that mean a lot to me. It's easy to make, serves a crowd, and is quick and tasty.

1 Winesap or Red Delicious apple, cored and small diced with skin left on

1 medium orange, seeded and cut into wedges with rind left on

4 tablespoons light brown sugar

1 cup freshly squeezed orange juice

½ cup Ole Smoky Apple Pie Moonshine

1 (750-ml) bottle dry red wine

2 cups club soda (or ginger ale, if you like a bit more sweetness)

Ice

Orange slices, for garnish

Combine the fruit with the brown sugar in a large pitcher. Muddle these together using the end of a large wooden spoon. Add the orange juice and moonshine and muddle again. Add the red wine and stir to blend. Add the club soda to taste. If needed, adjust the flavor by adding more orange juice. Add ice and stir a final time. Serve cold in mason jars with additional orange slices.

TWISTED OLD FASHIONED

SERVES 1

Meet the Twisted Old Fashioned, which uses our Ole Smoky Mango Habanero instead of regular whiskey. It's spicy, sweet, and a little bit naughty. Enjoy!

½ teaspoon sugar

3 dashes bitters

1 teaspoon water

Ice

2½ ounces Ole Smoky Mango Habanero Whiskey

Orange twist, for garnish

In a lowball glass, combine the sugar, bitters, and water. Stir to incorporate until the sugar is mostly dissolved. Fill the glass with ice, and slowly add the Ole Smoky Mango Habanero Whiskey. Gently stir to combine. Rub the orange twist along the rim and twist over the glass before serving.

THE SMOKY MOUNTAIN SHOT

SERVES 1

This shot hits the spot if you have a sweet tooth. With Ole Smoky Tennessee Mud, a sweet and creamy, chocolate-flavored liqueur, mixed with our Salty Caramel Whiskey and a mountain of whipped cream on top, who needs dessert?

½ ounce Ole Smoky Tennessee Mud

½ ounce Ole Smoky Salty Caramel Whiskey

Whipped cream

Mix the mud and whiskey together. Serve in a large shot glass, top with a mountain of whipped cream, and enjoy!

CHAPTER FOUR
DIPS

Oh, Tennessee River and a mountain man,
We get together anytime we can
Oh, Tennessee River and a mountain man,
We play together in Mother Nature's band

Tennessee River by Randy Owen

MANGO HABANERO SALSA

We can't grow mango in the Smoky Mountains, but this salsa is one of our favorites nonetheless. A fresh, zesty topping for fish tacos, grilled shrimp, or grilled chicken, this salsa aims to please all palates.

2 mangoes, peeled and diced

1 red pepper, deseeded and small diced

1 small red onion, small diced

1 habanero pepper, deseeded and small diced

2 tablespoons finely chopped fresh cilantro

Juice of one lime

1 tablespoon Ole Smoky Mango Habanero Whiskey

Tortilla chips, for serving

Mix all the ingredients together in a bowl. Chill for 30 minutes before serving to let the flavors meld. Serve with tortilla chips, or maybe even over a block of softened cream cheese if you need to cut down the heat a bit.

KICKIN' BUFFALO CHICKEN DIP
SERVES 10

In the South, Saturdays throughout the fall are reserved for tailgating at football games. Our Tennessee blood runs orange. This dip is a staple for the tens of thousands of fans pre-gaming around Neyland Stadium. Whether you love or hate the Tennessee Orange, you can't go wrong with this dish to fire you up for the big game. This goes well with celery sticks, corn chips, or French bread.

2 (8-ounce) packages cream cheese, room temperature

¼ cup hot sauce (I like Tabasco.)

½ cup buffalo sauce of your choice

½ cup ranch dressing of your choice

2 tablespoons Ole Smoky White Lightnin' Moonshine

2 cups shredded cooked chicken (I use rotisserie.)

2 cups shredded sharp cheddar cheese

½ teaspoon salt

½ teaspoon freshly ground black pepper

1 cup blue cheese crumbles

2 tablespoons chives, finely chopped

Celery sticks, corn chips, or slices of French bread, for serving

Preheat the oven to 350°F. Combine all the ingredients except the blue cheese crumbles and chives in a large bowl and mix well. Put in a rectangular 9 by 13-inch baking dish and bake, covered with aluminum foil, for 20 minutes, or until hot and bubbly.

Uncover, add the blue cheese crumbles, and broil for 5 minutes. Sprinkle with chives and serve with celery sticks, corn chips, or French bread.

PIMENTO CHEESE
SERVES 6

Pimento cheese reigns supreme in the cuisine of the South. It's a dip, a topping, a spread, even a relish at times. This versatile dish goes well with veggies, crackers, and even grilled burgers. It's fabulous in a grilled pimento cheese sandwich and an excellent topping for a Tennessee Whiskey Burger (page 92).

16 ounces freshly grated sharp cheddar cheese

1 (8-ounce) package cream cheese, softened

½ to ¾ cup mayonnaise

¼ cup diced pimientos, drained

½ teaspoon salt

¼ teaspoon freshly ground black pepper

¼ teaspoon garlic powder

¼ teaspoon dried onion flakes

¼ teaspoon red pepper flakes

Crackers or vegetable crudités, for serving

Combine the cheddar cheese and cream cheese, as well as possible, in a medium bowl. You can use an electric mixer, but I prefer to do it by hand. Stir in all the other ingredients and be sure they are well distributed throughout the mixture. You may need to add a little more mayonnaise if your dip seems too dry.

Store in an airtight container and refrigerate for at least 2 hours before serving, so the flavors can really set. Serve with crackers or vegetable crudités.

CHAPTER FIVE
SOUTHERN BREADS

Oh they call it that ole mountain dew
And them that refuse it are few
I'll shut up my mug if you fill up my jug
With some good ole mountain dew

Mountain Dew by Scott Wiseman and Bascom Lunsford

REAL CORN BREAD
SERVES 6 TO 8

My daughter Elli loves corn bread more than any other food. She will eat it anytime but insists on it for her birthday. I call this corn bread REAL because there are so many sweet, cakey versions out there that bear the name and don't deserve it. If you don't have a cast-iron skillet, please go buy one before cooking this recipe. Nothing else will do it justice and produce the golden-brown crust that makes this recipe a home run.

1 cup coarsely ground cornmeal (not a mix, I prefer stone ground)

1 cup all-purpose flour

¾ teaspoon salt

1 tablespoon baking powder

1 egg

1 cup whole milk

¼ cup unsalted butter, softened

2 tablespoons ghee, for cast-iron skillet

Butter and honey, for serving

Place a 10-inch, well-seasoned cast-iron skillet in your oven and preheat to 425°F. Combine the cornmeal, flour, salt, and baking powder together in a medium bowl. I like to use a fork or pastry blender to turn the dry ingredients over and over to be sure they're mixed and sifted.

Crack the egg into a small bowl and whisk it a bit. Add the milk to the egg and then whisk again lightly. Mix the butter into the dry ingredients, using a fork or pastry blender to be sure it's mixed in well. Don't add the egg and milk yet.

Once your oven is preheated, open it and add the ghee to the very hot cast-iron pan. Close the oven and let the ghee sit in the skillet for 1 to 2 minutes to heat to nearly sizzling.

Now it's time to mix the egg-milk mixture into the dry ingredients. Do this thoroughly and quickly, being sure not to overmix. Open the oven with an oven mitt on one hand, in case you need to pull the hot skillet toward you, and pour the mixture directly into the sizzling hot skillet of ghee. Smooth it out and close the oven. Bake for 20 to 24 minutes, until golden brown. Serve immediately with butter and honey.

BUTTERMILK BISCUITS
MAKES 8 TO 10 BISCUITS

When I was younger, I couldn't start the day without a biscuit for breakfast. They are the most comforting of all comfort foods. Flaky, light, and baked to a perfect golden brown, buttermilk biscuits are a welcome addition to any table.

2 cups all-purpose flour

¼ teaspoon baking soda

1 tablespoon baking powder

1 teaspoon kosher salt

6 tablespoons cold, unsalted butter, cubed

1 cup buttermilk

Preheat the oven to 450°F. In the bowl of a food processor, place the flour, baking soda, baking powder, and salt and pulse a couple times quickly to combine the dry ingredients well. Add the cold butter to the bowl and pulse for a few seconds 2 or 3 times until the butter is the size of tiny pebbles or frozen peas. Add the buttermilk and pulse quickly once or twice, until just combined. This is a very important step, because if you overmix, you will have tough biscuits.

Turn the dough out onto a floured board and pat it out (I don't roll it) into roughly a 9 by 13-inch rectangle that is about ½ inch thick. Next, fold the dough over itself 4 to 6 times, and gently pat it until it's about 1 inch thick. Using a round biscuit cutter, sized from 1 to 2½ inches in diameter, cut your biscuits out and put them onto a baking sheet.

If you let the sides of the biscuits touch each other, you'll have softer-sided biscuits. If you separate them, the biscuits will all be a little crunchier on the sides. This is a personal preference and totally up to you. Bake for 11 minutes, or until golden brown.

SOUTHERN SPOONBREAD
SERVES 4 TO 6

Almost every Sunday as a child, Joe's family lunch included a healthy portion of this corn specialty. Before the main event, a small dish of spoonbread was served as a weekly treat.

3 tablespoons unsalted butter, plus more for the baking dish and serving

4 eggs, separated

3 cups whole milk, divided

2 tablespoons Ole Smoky Original Corn Moonshine

1 cup cornmeal (stone ground)

¼ teaspoon baking powder

1½ teaspoons salt

Honey, for serving

Preheat the oven to 350°F. Use an extra tablespoon of butter to grease an 8-inch square baking dish. Place the egg whites in a medium bowl, add a pinch of salt, and beat until stiff peaks form. Set aside.

In a medium mixing bowl, add 1 cup milk, the Original Corn Moonshine, and the cornmeal. Stir well to combine.

In a heavy-bottomed, medium saucepan, heat the remaining 2 cups of milk until lightly boiling and bubbling near the sides of the pan. Add the cornmeal-milk mixture. Cook on low, stirring constantly, until the cornmeal starts to thicken and pulls away from the sides of the saucepan, about 10 minutes.

Remove from the heat, add 3 tablespoons of butter, the baking powder, and salt to the cornmeal mixture, and stir well.

In a small bowl, beat the egg yolks, and then add a tablespoon of the warm cornmeal mixture to the yolks, and stir. Add one more tablespoon and stir again. Finally, add the yolk mixture to the cornmeal mixture and stir well.

Fold the beaten egg whites into the cornmeal mixture until combined. Pour the mixture into the prepared baking dish and bake for 50 minutes, until a toothpick inserted in the center comes out clean and the top is puffed up and browned. Serve immediately with butter and honey.

SKILLET-FRIED CORNPONES
MAKES ROUGHLY 8 CORNPONES

Cornpones are very similar in composition to corn bread, but they are fried in smaller cakes in a cast-iron skillet. Since corn was such a cornerstone of the Appalachian diet, it makes sense that there are many ways to cook it. Cornpones are great with everything, from Ramps & Eggs (page 125) for brunch to my Chicken Fried Steak (page 82) and shining Southern Collard Greens (page 100) for dinner. They also stand alone as dessert with butter, honey, and jam.

2 cups coarsely ground cornmeal

1 teaspoon kosher salt

2 teaspoons baking powder

1 cup whole milk

2 tablespoons Ole Smoky Original Corn Moonshine

2 tablespoons reserved bacon fat

2 tablespoons canola oil

Heat a 12-inch cast-iron skillet over low heat to get it hot and ready to fry. Combine the cornmeal, salt, and baking powder in a medium bowl and stir well. Add the milk and moonshine and stir again until combined. Be careful not to overmix. Carefully place bacon fat and canola oil into the skillet. Once the fat is hot, drop large spoonfuls of the cornmeal mixture into the skillet 2 to 3 inches apart. Fry until golden brown, 2 to 3 minutes, flip, then fry until golden brown on the other side, 2 to 3 minutes more. Serve immediately.

DROP BISCUITS

MAKES 10 BISCUITS

The difference between drop biscuits and rolled biscuits is that drop biscuits have more milk added to the dough mixture. The dough is so moist, in fact, that it can't be rolled or even kneaded, thereby necessitating dropping the dough directly onto the baking sheet. Drop biscuits also don't rise much, and they are more rustic looking, too.

2 cups all-purpose flour

1 tablespoon baking powder

1 teaspoon sugar

1 teaspoon salt

¾ cup (1½ sticks) cold, unsalted butter, cut into squares

1¼ cups whole milk

Preheat the oven to 425°F. Line a rectangular baking sheet with parchment paper. In the bowl of a food processor, mix the flour, baking powder, sugar, and salt together. Add the butter and pulse until your mixture looks a bit like pebbly sand. Add one cup of milk first, then check the dough before adding more. You want the mixture to be wet, but not runny. Add milk one tablespoon at a time until you have the right consistency.

Using a large spoon, drop the dough in 8 to 10 mounds on your baking sheet, about 2 inches apart. Bake for about 20 minutes, or until a toothpick inserted in the center comes out clean. Biscuits are best eaten straight out of the oven while they're hot, but if you have leftovers, these will keep in an airtight container for a couple of days; in fact, you can even freeze them! I prefer to reheat them in a toaster oven to keep their outsides crunchy.

continued

VARIATION: CHEDDAR, GARLIC, & CHIVE DROP BISCUITS

I find that my family prefers drop biscuits most when I make them like this. All you do is make the dough as stated above, but before dropping the biscuits onto the sheet, add ¾ cup shredded sharp cheddar cheese, 2 cloves minced garlic, and ¼ cup minced chives to the mixture. Then drop them onto a baking sheet as directed. I especially like to brush this version with a small amount of melted butter when they are finished. They are SO savory and the perfect accompaniment to any soup or chowder.

CHAPTER SIX
SALADS

In my Tennessee mountain home
Life is as peaceful as a baby's sigh
In my Tennessee mountain home
Crickets sing in the fields nearby

My Tennessee Mountain Home by Dolly Parton

24-HOUR SALAD
SERVES 6 TO 8

This traditional southern salad was served at nearly every family picnic and holiday of Joe's young life. It's called 24-Hour Salad because it's best when made a day ahead. I hope it becomes a family favorite for your crew, too! It's constructed in a glass bowl to reveal the beautiful layers.

8 cups torn iceberg lettuce

1½ cups celery, small diced

2 medium-sized green peppers, deseeded and small diced

1 medium red onion, small diced

1 (10 or 12-ounce) bag frozen peas, thawed and drained

1 cup mayonnaise

1 cup sour cream

1 teaspoon minced fresh dill

1 tablespoon minced fresh parsley

Juice from 1 lemon

½ teaspoon freshly ground black pepper

1 teaspoon kosher salt

½ pound bacon, cooked and crumbled

2 hard-boiled eggs, chopped

1 cup shredded cheddar cheese

Place the iceberg lettuce in a large, glass bowl (the see-through bowl is for presentation because the layers of this salad are gorgeous). Start layering with the celery on top of the lettuce, then the green pepper, red onion, and finishing with the peas.

In a separate bowl, whisk together the mayonnaise, sour cream, dill, parsley, lemon juice, and pepper and salt. Pour over the top of your veggies. Then layer the bacon, eggs, and cheese over the top. Cover and chill for 12 to 24 hours before serving.

SLAW
SERVES 6

I would eat this coleslaw every day. It is THAT good. I like my coleslaw without sugar, so know that before you make it. This is a salty, vinegary coleslaw that gets its creamy base from mayo and sour cream. It's also garlicky, so beware of that, in case you want to cut the amount of garlic in half. Serve in a family-sized bowl.

½ cup mayonnaise

½ cup sour cream

¼ cup white wine vinegar

2 garlic cloves, minced

1 teaspoon celery seed

¾ teaspoon kosher salt

2 (14-ounce) packages shredded coleslaw

Use a whisk to combine the mayonnaise, sour cream, vinegar, garlic, celery seed, and salt together well in a family-sized bowl. Once combined, add the coleslaw, and mix well. Chill for at least 1 hour before serving.

SPRING GREENS WITH FENNEL & RAW HONEY VINAIGRETTE

SERVES 6 TO 8

When you are cooking out of a garden, as many in Appalachia do, salad choices are largely based on whatever happens to be in season. I dedicate my love of leaves and greens to my mother, and I hope this salad honors her amazing garden and the bounty that grows from it.

Dressing

- ¼ cup freshly squeezed orange juice
- 3 tablespoons freshly squeezed lemon juice
- 2 tablespoons raw honey
- 2 tablespoons olive oil
- ¾ teaspoon kosher salt
- ½ teaspoon freshly ground black pepper

Salad

- 1 fennel bulb, trimmed, halved, and cored, and then sliced thinly lengthwise
- 2 tablespoons fresh dill, chopped
- 1 head butter lettuce, torn into bite-size pieces
- 1 head red leaf lettuce, torn into bite-size pieces
- 1 head bibb lettuce, torn into bite-size pieces

Garnish

- 1 tablespoon bee pollen
- ⅓ cup toasted walnuts

To make the dressing, combine the orange juice, lemon juice, honey, and olive oil in a small bowl. Whisk well and add the salt and pepper. Whisk again, check for taste, and set aside.

Combine all the salad ingredients together in a large bowl. Add the dressing and toss well. Sprinkle the top of the salad with the bee pollen and walnuts and serve.

CUCUMBERS & ONIONS
SERVES 6

Simple and delicious, a classic southern side dish that is reminiscent of summer and some of the most reliable offerings from any garden. One of my favorite cucumber-and-onion salads is from the Pancake Pantry in Gatlinburg. It's a staple on their tables during the lunch rush, but my version is a bit different, as it omits the sour cream.

3 cucumbers, peeled partially in 3 or 4 long strips to create a striped cucumber

1 medium purple onion or sweet yellow onion

1 tablespoon chopped fresh dill

1 teaspoon sugar

½ teaspoon kosher salt

½ teaspoon freshly ground black pepper

½ cup apple cider vinegar

Juice from half a lemon

¼ cup olive oil

Slice the cucumber in thin rounds and place in a large bowl. Peel the onion. Slice in half and then into thin, ⅛ inch slices. Add the dill to the bowl.

In another small bowl, mix the sugar, salt, pepper, apple cider vinegar, lemon juice, and olive oil. Once combined, pour over the cucumbers and onions and mix well. Refrigerate for at least an hour before serving.

BLT SALAD WITH HOMEMADE BUTTERMILK RANCH DRESSING & GARLICKY CROUTONS

SERVES 6 TO 8

I'll start by stating my belief that all homemade ranch dressing should have buttermilk in it. Like a true southern accent, it's got a twang that can't be mimicked. This is one of the best, most flavorful salads that I make on a regular basis. Dressings are kind of my thing, and I firmly believe that homemade is worth the time and energy. It's just so easy to make your own, and they taste that much better.

Ranch Dressing

½ cup sour cream or Greek yogurt

½ cup buttermilk

¼ cup mayonnaise

2 garlic cloves, minced

¾ teaspoon salt

½ teaspoon freshly ground black pepper

⅛ teaspoon cayenne

1 teaspoon Worcestershire sauce

2 teaspoons fresh dill, minced

2 tablespoons fresh chives, finely chopped

Juice from half a lemon

Garlicky Croutons

1 loaf French bread or any crusty bread

1 teaspoon garlic powder

½ teaspoon salt

¼ cup olive oil

Salad

2 cups halved cherry tomatoes

Salt

2 heads romaine lettuce, washed and shredded

Handful of Garlicky Croutons

1 (16-ounce) package bacon, cooked and chopped

To make the dressing, add all the ingredients to a bowl and whisk vigorously. Store chilled in a mason jar up to 3 or 4 days.

To make the croutons, preheat the oven to 275°F. Cut bread into bite-sized pieces, and place in a large bowl with the garlic powder and salt. Mix together, trying to coat the bread in the powder. Add olive oil, trying not to soak the bread, but enough to have it glistening and sticky so it accepts the salt and garlic powder. Transfer the bread to a baking sheet and bake for 10 minutes, or until golden brown; check at 5 minutes and toss the pieces so that they brown evenly. Croutons will keep in an airtight container up to 10 days.

To make the salad, place the tomatoes in a bowl. Sprinkle with ¼ to ½ teaspoon salt, and let them sit about 5 minutes to release some juices. Combine the lettuce, tomatoes, croutons, and bacon in a family-sized salad bowl. Top with the ranch dressing, toss, and serve.

POTATO & GREEN BEAN SALAD

SERVES 6 TO 8

This potato salad is less creamy than some but full of flavor due to the bacon and tangy dressing. Potato salad is something that everyone makes differently, so with a million versions out there, I offer this one as a solid, mayo-free option.

Salad

8-10 new potatoes, skin on

1 pound fresh green beans, rinsed and trimmed into 1-inch pieces, cooked al dente

1 medium red onion, small diced

8 strips bacon, cooked and coarsely chopped

¼ cup fresh flat leaf parsley, chopped

Vinaigrette

¼ cup balsamic vinegar

2 cloves garlic, minced

2 tablespoons fresh lemon juice

2 tablespoons Dijon mustard

½ teaspoon Worcestershire sauce

½ cup olive oil

¾ teaspoon salt

½ teaspoon freshly ground black pepper

To make the salad, start by cooking the potatoes and green beans. For the potatoes, bring a large pot of water to boil over high heat. Add the potatoes, whole with skins on, and cook for 12 to 15 minutes, until fork tender. Remove from the water to let cool. Cut into large chunks, leaving the skins on. For the beans, boil them in salted water in a medium-large saucepan for about 4 minutes, drain, and transfer to a bowl of ice water. Drain again and pat the beans dry. Gently combine the cooled potatoes and green beans, onion, bacon, and parsley in a large bowl.

To make the vinaigrette, whisk all the ingredients together in a separate, smaller bowl. Pour the vinaigrette over the salad ingredients and stir together. Serve chilled or at room temperature.

A VERY GREEN SALAD WITH CILANTRO-CIDER DRESSING

SERVES 6

For those bored with their typical salads, this will be a wonderfully tasty discovery. The zesty, tangy flavors in this fresh salad will surprise and please most palates. This dressing ends up being much creamier than you would expect, and people are usually shocked when I tell them the ingredients. It makes for a very mellow, beautiful flavor that I think you'll love!

Salad

1 large head romaine lettuce, washed, dried, and hand-torn

1 cucumber, peeled, seeded, and medium diced

5 large celery sticks, trimmed and small diced

1 bunch green onions, both green and white parts, trimmed and thinly sliced

Dressing

Leaves from 20-25 stems of fresh cilantro

½ cup olive oil

¾ cup apple cider vinegar

1 small white onion, finely chopped

1 teaspoon kosher salt

½ teaspoon freshly ground black pepper

To make the salad, combine the lettuce, cucumber, celery, and green onions in a large salad bowl.

To make the dressing, add the cilantro and olive oil to a blender and puree. Next, add the vinegar, onion, salt, and pepper and blend again for a full 20 to 30 seconds, until all are puréed. This recipe makes enough dressing for two whole salads, and the dressing will keep up to 3 days in the refrigerator.

CHAPTER SEVEN

SOUPS AND STEWS

The Tennessee Stud was long and lean
The color of the sun and his eyes were green
He had the nerve and he had the blood
There never was a horse like Tennessee Stud

Tennessee Stud by Jimmy Driftwood

MOONSHINE CHILI
SERVES 10 TO 12

Chili is one of our family's favorite meals. You can make it so many ways and add so many different veggies or beans to increase the protein content and make it healthier. I like adding the masa flour because it complements the flavor of the corn whiskey and helps make the chili more hearty.

I firmly believe that chili is better when it cooks for a few hours, and it's almost always better the day after you make it. The following instructions allow for only an hour and a half to make the chili, which is really all you need to assemble and cook it. However, letting it simmer and stew longer will enhance its flavor. If you aren't going to be near the stove so you can stir it, put the cooked portion in a slow cooker and leave it on low all day. Also, remember that the longer it cooks on the stove, the more broth you'll need to add. Finally, this makes a huge pot of chili. I find that when I'm making chili, I'm either feeding a crowd or happy to have leftovers to freeze, so this amount works well for my family.

2½ to 3 pounds ground beef

1 tablespoon of ghee

4 bell peppers, small diced (I like using peppers of different colors.)

2 medium yellow onions, small diced

1 teaspoon cumin

½ teaspoon cayenne

2 teaspoons salt

1 teaspoon freshly ground black pepper

1 teaspoon paprika

¾ teaspoon oregano

5 tablespoons chili pepper powder

1 (29-ounce) can diced tomatoes

1 (29-ounce) can pinto beans, rinsed and drained

1 (29-ounce) can kidney beans, rinsed and drained

1 (15-ounce) can black beans, rinsed and drained

1 (15-ounce) can cannellini beans, rinsed and drained

1 (15-ounce) can water

2 quart boxes of beef broth (You'll use one in the main recipe and need to have another on hand in case you cook the chili for a few hours and need to add extra.)

2 teaspoons masa flour

½ cup Ole Smoky Original Corn Moonshine

continued

Brown the ground beef in a large pot over medium heat. Drain the grease, and set aside.

Using the same pot that you browned the meat in, add the ghee and sauté the peppers and onion for 8 minutes over medium heat, until the onion turns translucent. Add the cumin, cayenne, salt, pepper, paprika, oregano, and chili powder, and give it a good stir. Add the tomatoes in their juices, rinsed beans, water, and one quart of the beef broth. Mash the beans a bit with a handheld potato masher, not so much that you completely erase their shape, but rough them up a bit so that their flavor and inside texture are released into the broth. Cover and simmer over low heat for 30 minutes.

Mix the masa with a ½ cup of warm water first, and then add it to the chili. It adds an earthy and natural flavor while also thickening the broth. Let simmer 10 minutes. Add the Ole Smoky Original Corn Moonshine, and let simmer 10 to 15 minutes more before serving. Remember that if you leave this on the stove awhile, you'll need to add more beef broth as it cooks down.

CHICKEN & RICE CURE-ALL SOUP

SERVES 6

I'm a busy mom, so I take all the help I can get when making chicken soup. I rarely roast my own meat, preferring instead to buy a rotisserie chicken and pick the meat off the bones. It cuts down your cooking time significantly and still makes for a soup that tastes slow-cooked and amazing. I do, however, choose to take the long route for my broth. I often keep the bones from the rotisserie chicken and put them in a slow cooker with some celery, onions, and carrots for up to 24 hours. I strain off the fat and freeze that broth for the next time I need it.

2 tablespoons ghee

¼ cup olive oil

4 medium celery ribs, small diced

5 medium carrots, small diced

2 medium yellow onions, small diced

1 teaspoon chopped fresh thyme

1 cup uncooked brown rice

3 quarts chicken stock or broth (I usually try to use at least one and a half quarts homemade stock, which makes all the difference.)

1½ teaspoons salt

1 teaspoon freshly ground black pepper

½ teaspoon turmeric

1 bay leaf

1 rotisserie chicken meat, chopped

¼ cup chopped flat leaf parsley

5 ounces fresh spinach, chopped

In a large stockpot, heat the ghee and olive oil over medium heat. Add the celery, carrots, onion, and thyme, and cook until the vegetables soften, 8 to 10 minutes. Add the brown rice and stir well. Sauté the rice about 2 minutes, lightly roasting it until it pops a bit. Add the broth, salt, pepper, turmeric, and bay leaf. Stir together and let this simmer over low heat for at least 40 minutes.

Add the chicken, parsley, and spinach and cook for 10 minutes more. At this point, the soup is ready to serve. However, the longer a soup sits on the stove, the better it's going to taste. I often try to make mine early in the day and leave it on the stove for 4 or 5 hours, or if I'm going to be away from home and can't stir it, I put it in a slow cooker on low. No one wants their soup stuck to the bottom of the pot! Remember that if you do continue to cook it, you'll need to add extra broth since it will cook down.

BEEF STEW
SERVES 6

There are few things heartier or more comforting than a well-made beef stew. This stew is a Baker family standard. It uses both wine and moonshine, and I think you'll be pleasantly surprised at the subtleties they add to the flavor profile.

1½ pounds beef chuck roast, cut into 1-inch cubes

1 teaspoon kosher salt

½ teaspoon freshly ground black pepper

¼ cup all-purpose flour

5 teaspoons ghee or vegetable oil, divided

2 medium yellow onions, medium chopped

4 cloves garlic, minced

2 tablespoons Ole Smoky Original Corn Moonshine

1 cup dry red wine

3 sprigs thyme, leaves picked off and minced

6 cups beef broth

2 bay leaves, whole

6 celery stalks, cut into 1-inch pieces

8 carrots, peeled and cut into ½-inch rounds

8-10 new potatoes, cut into 1-inch cubes

Season the cubed beef with salt and pepper, then coat with the flour (I like to use a plastic bag to shake them all together). In a large Dutch oven, add 3 teaspoons of ghee or vegetable oil and brown the beef on all sides over medium heat. You may need to do this in two batches.

Remove all the beef from the pan and add the remaining 2 teaspoons of ghee or oil. Sauté the onion and garlic until softened, about 3 minutes. Add the Ole Smoky Original Corn Moonshine and wine. Use a wooden spoon to scrape the pan and loosen any brown bits stuck to the bottom.

Next add the thyme, beef broth, and bay leaves. Put the browned beef back into the Dutch oven and bring to a boil over high heat. Decrease the heat to low and simmer for about 1 hour, skimming the broth every 20 minutes or so. After an hour, add the celery and carrots, and cook for 20 minutes more.

Finally, add the potatoes and cook for an additional 30 minutes, or until all vegetables are fork tender. If the stew cooks down, add more liquid, either beef broth or water. Taste for seasoning, and add more salt and pepper as needed.

CREAMY POTATO SOUP
SERVES 6 TO 8

From the time I was a little girl, I loved creamy potato soup. I remember visiting my grandparents in Fire Island, New York, when it was a cold and windy day in the fall. We trekked to the top of the lighthouse, where our view of the Great South Bay was crystal clear. When we came home, there was potato soup on the stove, the aroma of dill and onion filled the air, and I ate until my stomach nearly burst. Something about this special soup always makes me nostalgic. The Cheddar Chive Drop Biscuits (page 50) pair well with this recipe.

3 tablespoons ghee

1 yellow onion, small diced

3 medium carrots, small diced

3 stalks celery, small diced

6 russet potatoes, peeled and small diced

4 to 6 cups chicken broth (You need enough to cover the potatoes by 1 inch once they are in the pot.)

3 tablespoons unsalted butter

⅓ cup all-purpose flour

1½ cups milk

½ cup heavy cream

1 cup sour cream

2 tablespoons chopped fresh dill

1½ teaspoons kosher salt

1 teaspoon freshly ground black pepper

Green onions or chives, chopped, for garnish

In a large Dutch oven, add the ghee and sauté the onion, carrots, and celery over medium heat until the onion is translucent and softened, 6 to 8 minutes. Add the potatoes, and toss all together. Sauté for 3 minutes more. Add the chicken broth and bring to a boil over high heat. Lower the heat and simmer until the potatoes are fork tender, 12 to 14 minutes.

Meanwhile, in a separate pan, melt the butter over medium heat. Add the flour and whisk constantly while it cooks for 2 or 3 minutes. Add the milk and cream and continue whisking until thickened.

Finally, stir the creamy mixture into the potato soup base. Remove half of the soup and place in a blender or food processor. Purée until smooth, then pour back into the Dutch oven. Stir in the sour cream, dill, salt, and pepper. Serve with chopped green onions or chives sprinkled over the top.

EVERYTHING BUT THE KITCHEN SINK VEGGIE SOUP
SERVES 6 TO 8

Do you ever go to the grocery store or farmers' market and over-purchase? It's easy to be in awe of nature's bounty. That happens to me a lot, and I always seem to have leftovers. So, I've been working with a few recipes to try to combine veggies into a healthy, beautiful soup that helps clean out your refrigerator and pantry, too. I'm using more and more coconut milk in my everyday cooking, but half-and-half or whipping cream works well if you're of a dairy persuasion. This recipe is an excellent tonic to sip on if you're ill or if you drank a little too much shine the night before.

2 medium onions, coarsely chopped, small enough to sauté

4 cloves garlic, coarsely chopped

6 to 8 stalks celery, leaves left on, coarsely chopped

2 bunches of broccoli with main large stem removed, coarsely chopped

½ teaspoon red pepper flakes

1 teaspoon kosher salt

½ teaspoon freshly ground black pepper

6 to 8 waxy white potatoes, skins on and medium diced

8 cups chicken broth

Water

2 (14-ounce) cans full-fat coconut milk

1 (5-ounce) box arugula leaves

¼ cup sliced almonds, toasted, for garnish

In a large stockpot over medium heat, sauté the onion and garlic for 5 minutes, or until the onions are soft. Add the celery and sauté for 5 minutes more. Add the broccoli heads and sauté until they are a very bright green, 3 to 4 minutes. Add the red pepper flakes, salt, and pepper. Next, add the potatoes, the chicken broth, and water, as needed to cover the vegetables by about 1 inch. Bring to a boil and simmer uncovered for 15 to 20 minutes, or until veggies are tender.

Remove from the heat, add the coconut milk, and stir to mix. Blend the soup using an immersion blender, adding the fresh arugula one handful at a time. Blend after each addition until pureed. The fresh arugula gives the soup a beautiful bright color and peppery twang. Rewarm in the stockpot over low heat, and serve with toasted almonds on top.

CHICKEN & DUMPLINGS
SERVES 6 TO 8

This is my husband's childhood favorite, and it makes an appearance at our house a few times a year. I love to make my dumplings with half-and-half, flour, and cornmeal. This gives them a rustic taste that is still light and fluffy. I also add copious amounts of veggies and herbs to this soup.

As a side note, many cooks who make chicken and dumplings the old-fashioned way roll out their dumpling dough and slice it into diamonds or cut it with a biscuit mold. This method makes for denser, yet thinner dumplings. My husband prefers these because it's how his Mamaw used to make them. For me, I like both varieties but prefer the version below with a more veggie-filled soup. Just don't overwork the dumpling dough and keep them small; try using a medium-sized melon baller to drop them in the pot.

Soup

2 tablespoons ghee

2 tablespoons olive oil

6 carrots, peeled and small diced

5 stalks celery, small diced

2 medium yellow onions, small diced

2 teaspoons minced fresh thyme

½ teaspoon turmeric

1 teaspoon poultry seasoning

1½ teaspoons kosher salt

1 teaspoon freshly ground black pepper

2 quarts chicken broth

Meat from 1 rotisserie chicken, cut into bite-sized pieces

1 (10 to 12-ounce) bag frozen peas

¼ cup chopped fresh flat leaf parsley

Dumplings

1½ cups all-purpose flour

½ cup coarse or medium-ground cornmeal

2 tablespoons baking powder

1½ teaspoons salt

½ teaspoon freshly ground black pepper

1 cup half-and-half

1 egg, beaten

To make the soup, place the ghee and olive oil in a large, 9-quart Dutch oven over medium heat. Sauté the carrot, celery, and onion for 8 to 10 minutes. Once softened, add the thyme, turmeric, poultry seasoning, salt, and pepper. Stir together and then add the chicken broth. Simmer for 30 minutes over low heat. Stir in the chicken, frozen peas, and parsley. Simmer for 10 minutes more over low heat.

To make the dumplings, first combine the flour, cornmeal, baking powder, salt, and pepper in a medium bowl. Then mix the half-and-half together with the beaten egg in a small bowl. Gently stir the cream and egg mixture into the flour mixture, being careful not to overmix it. Drop the dough by spoonfuls into the broth. Leave the lid off for 10 minutes while simmering, and then replace it and simmer for 10 minutes more. Serve and enjoy!

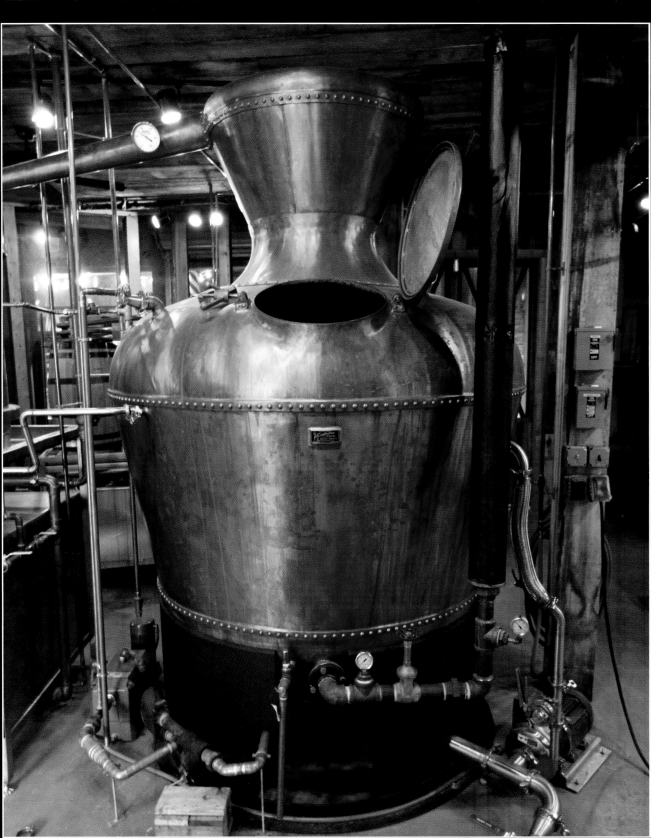

CHAPTER EIGHT

MAINS

If you'll be my Dixie chicken I'll be your Tennessee lamb
And we can walk together down in Dixieland
Down in Dixieland

Dixie Chicken by Lowell George & Martin Kibbee

WHISKEY BRISKET

SERVES 8 TO 10

My dear friend Julie is from Wyoming. Her family raises cattle and she makes some of the best beef you've ever tasted. I first tasted her brisket recipe at a party and was completely wowed by its tender, juicy flavor. I never saw five pounds of meat disappear so fast! People were eating it alone, on sandwiches, or beside mashed potatoes. It's really a versatile dish. My kids loved it so much that I asked for her brisket recipe and then doctored it up a bit with our Ole Smoky Straight Bourbon Tennessee Whiskey. I think you'll love the result!

5 pounds brisket

Salt

Freshly ground black pepper

2 teaspoons garlic salt

½ teaspoon cayenne

2 tablespoons Worcestershire

1 tablespoon liquid smoke

½ cup soy sauce

½ cup Ole Smoky Tennessee Straight Bourbon Whiskey

¼ cup maple syrup

½ teaspoon finely grated orange zest

Juice from 1 orange

2 tablespoons minced fresh thyme

2 tablespoons minced fresh oregano

2 tablespoons minced fresh parsley

2 tablespoons minced fresh rosemary

Trim the top layer of fat off the brisket to about ⅓ of an inch, and season the brisket generously with salt and pepper. Score the meat on both sides.

Combine the remaining ingredients in a large bowl. Transfer this mixture to a large turkey-basting bag, add the brisket, and seal tightly. Place the bag on a baking sheet in the refrigerator to marinate overnight.

The next morning, remove the meat from the bag and reserve the marinade. Transfer the meat to a large casserole dish and pour the reserved marinade on top and around it. Cover the dish tightly with aluminum foil and bake in the oven at 250°F for 8 to 10 hours.

Remove the meat from the pan and strain the juices into a small bowl. Shred the meat and set alongside the juices. If you're not serving a crowd, this dish will produce leftovers, and they freeze really well for up to 2 months.

BBQ PULLED PORK WITH APPLE PIE MOONSHINE

SERVES 8 TO 10

The base of this recipe is from a good friend of mine, Claudia Laffin, who is a personal chef at the Traveling Spoon in Asheville, North Carolina. When she heard I was writing a moonshine cookbook, she volunteered to experiment with our Ole Smoky Apple Pie Moonshine, and this recipe was born.

4 pounds pork shoulder or butt

3 teaspoons salt, plus extra for seasoning

1 teaspoon freshly ground black pepper, plus extra for seasoning

½ cup ketchup

½ cup chicken broth

½ cup Ole Smoky Apple Pie Moonshine

¼ cup light brown sugar

1 teaspoon Dijon mustard

1 teaspoon apple cider vinegar

2 medium yellow onions, chopped

Trim any excess fat off of the pork shoulder. Place in a slow cooker, sprinkle with salt and pepper, and rub them in to the skin.

Combine the rest of the ingredients in a small bowl and whisk well. Pour over the pork and cook on low for 9 to 10 hours or on high for 4 to 5 hours.

Using tongs, pull out the pork and onions and place in a large bowl to cool. Once cooled to the touch, shred the pork with two forks or your fingers. I like to chop the onions and put them back in with the pork, but you are welcome to toss them at this point if you'd rather have only meat in your final dish.

Skim the fat from the sauce left in the slow cooker; a large lettuce leaf works well to do this, or pour the sauce into a 4-cup fat separator and let that do the work. After the pork is shredded, pour half of the sauce over the pork and save the rest for serving. This dish freezes well for up to 2 months.

PORK CHOPS & BUTTERMILK GRAVY

SERVES 4

I make these pork chops whenever it's cold and dreary outside because they are warming and comforting, like soup. The gravy that you make with them is thinner than what's on a country fried steak, so don't be alarmed—it's supposed to be that way.

1½ cups all-purpose flour

2 tablespoons onion powder

2 tablespoons garlic powder

¾ teaspoon salt, plus extra for seasoning

½ teaspoon cayenne

½ teaspoon paprika

½ teaspoon freshly ground black pepper, plus extra for seasoning

4 boneless pork chops (You can use bone-in, but I like this best because it's easier for my kids to cut on their own.)

¼ cup canola oil

1 tablespoon ghee

2 cups chicken broth

1 cup buttermilk

2 tablespoons chopped fresh parsley

In a shallow baking dish, mix the flour, onion powder, garlic powder, salt, cayenne, paprika, and pepper. Reserve ½ cup of the seasoned flour for the gravy.

Pat the pork chops dry with paper towels, then season them on both sides with additional salt and pepper. Heat a large cast-iron skillet over medium heat. When warm, add the canola oil and ghee. Dredge the pork chops in the remaining seasoned flour to coat them. When the oil is hot, add the chops directly to the skillet. Cook for 3 to 5 minutes per side. Once golden brown, remove the chops to a paper towel-lined plate (don't worry yet about whether they are completely done).

Slowly add about ¼ cup of the reserved flour to the hot drippings. Whisk until a thick paste forms. Cook for 30 seconds to 1 minute, then add your chicken broth. Whisk vigorously. Once this mixture thickens enough to stick to the back of a spoon, add the buttermilk, and stir to blend.

Return the pork chops to the skillet and cover. Cook for 5 to 10 minutes more on a low simmer. Taste the gravy to be sure there's enough salt, and season to taste. Top with the chopped parsley and serve.

MOONSHINE CHICKEN
SERVES 5

This is definitely not your run-of-the-mill chicken dish. Moonshine Chicken spices things up with the sweet, hot flavors of moonshine and cayenne. This juicy chicken will make fans of everyone who eats it.

Chicken

5 chicken breasts, bone in and skin left on

Salt

Freshly ground black pepper

Butter Sauce

½ cup unsalted butter, melted

¼ teaspoon cayenne

¼ teaspoon salt

¼ teaspoon freshly ground pepper

Moonshine-Mustard Sauce

½ cup Dijon mustard

¼ cup maple syrup

2 tablespoons Ole Smoky Blue Flame Moonshine

1 teaspoon minced fresh rosemary

To prepare the chicken, preheat the oven to 375°F. Generously season the chicken breasts on both sides with salt and pepper.

To prepare the butter sauce, mix the melted butter, cayenne, salt, and pepper in small bowl. Rub the butter sauce all over the chicken breasts and spoon under the skin. Let sit on the counter for 5 minutes while making the moonshine-mustard sauce.

To make the moonshine sauce, whisk together the Dijon mustard, maple syrup, Ole Smoky Blue Flame Moonshine, and rosemary in a small bowl. Rub the mustard sauce all over the breasts, again spooning the mixture under the skin.

Bake the chicken, breast side up, for 55 minutes, or until meat thermometer reads 165°F. This chicken pairs well with the Skillet-Fried Green Beans (page 107) and Fried Potatoes (page 99).

CHICKEN FRIED STEAK
SERVES 4

Chicken fried steak was my all-time favorite as a child. I loved the crispy outside and the yummy gravy that surrounded it. What's not to love about that? Despite the name, this dish contains no chicken. Since the cooking method is very similar to the way we make fried chicken, the name was born. Some people call this country fried steak, but it's essentially the same thing!

Steak

4 (4 to 6-ounce) beef cube steaks

2 teaspoons salt, plus extra for seasoning

¾ teaspoon freshly ground black pepper, plus extra for seasoning

2½ cups all-purpose flour

1 teaspoon paprika

½ teaspoon cayenne

2 cups buttermilk

2 eggs, beaten

2 tablespoons ghee

¼ cup canola oil

Gravy

4 cups milk

⅓ to ½ cup seasoned flour

To prepare the steaks, pound them out to about ¼-inch thickness. Season them generously with salt and pepper on both sides. Mix the flour with 2 teaspoons salt, ¾ teaspoon black pepper, paprika, and cayenne. Reserve ½ cup of the seasoned flour for the gravy. Put the remaining flour mixture in a shallow-bottomed baking dish.

Mix the buttermilk with the eggs in another shallow-bottomed baking dish, and set this beside the seasoned flour.

Warm a cast-iron skillet over medium heat and, once hot, add the ghee and canola oil. You don't want this to smoke. If it does, you need to turn the heat down. Dredge the cube steak, one piece at a time, in the milk and egg mixture, then in the flour, and set immediately in the hot pan. Cook the meat roughly 3 minutes per side, then set on a paper towel-lined plate. You can keep the steaks warm in a low oven or warming drawer, or just use a piece of aluminum foil to cover them on the plate.

When finished cooking the steak, pour the remaining grease into a heat-safe bowl. You'll need ¼ cup of the grease and pan drippings for the gravy.

To make the gravy, use the same skillet you did to cook the steak. Return your reserved ¼ cup of grease back to the pan and warm over medium heat. Once the oil is hot, sprinkle ⅓ to ½ cup of the reserved seasoned flour into the pan. Stir the flour to mix well with the grease and drippings. You know you've added enough flour when the mixture in the pan is a thick paste, much like the consistency of peanut butter. This is your roux. Cook for about 1 minute before you stir in the milk.

Add the milk to the flour mixture, whisking continuously. Cook for 5 to 10 minutes, whisking the entire time. As the gravy thickens, add more salt and pepper to taste. I usually use about 1½ teaspoons more of kosher salt, and ½ teaspoon of freshly ground black pepper.

To serve, plate a piece of the fried steak and smother it with the gravy. Enjoy!

20-POINT SPAGHETTI WITH MOONSHINE TOMATO SAUCE

SERVES 6

You guessed it, this dish is clearly not Appalachian, but it is a family favorite. It tastes great all the same, and is similar to a vodka cream pasta. At one point or another, my dad coached each of his six children in basketball. We come by our competitive spirit honestly. My dad took such pride in cooking this dish and called it his 20-point spaghetti recipe. He liked to believe we would score 20 points or more if we ate this lucky meal. Tomatoes and carbs were the secret, and I've doctored it up even more with a bit of moonshine, but it's essentially the same. I hope it brings you success on or off the court.

1 teaspoon olive oil

1 tablespoon ghee

1 medium yellow onion, finely chopped

3 garlic cloves, minced

2 teaspoons chopped fresh oregano

2 (28-ounce) cans whole tomatoes, shredded by hand (Careful, they squirt! Use a deep bowl.)

2 teaspoons kosher salt

½ teaspoon freshly ground black pepper

½ teaspoon red pepper flakes

1 cup chicken stock

½ cup Ole Smoky White Lightnin' Moonshine

16 ounces spaghetti (All dried spaghetti is not created equal. I like De Cecco.)

½ cup heavy cream

16 leaves basil, torn by hand

Heat a large stockpot over medium heat. Add the olive oil, ghee, and onion. When the onions start to turn translucent, 4 to 5 minutes, add the garlic. After about 1 minute more, stir in the oregano, tomatoes, salt, pepper, and red pepper flakes. Give the sauce a stir, add the chicken stock or broth and the Ole Smoky White Lightnin' Moonshine, and bring to a boil.

Decrease the heat and simmer until the liquid is reduced by half. During this time, mash the tomatoes as they cook to continue releasing their juices and pulp. I like to use a potato masher. Also during this time, cook your pasta in salted water. When you drain it, save ½ cup of the pasta water to add to the sauce.

Once the pasta is cooked, add the cream and the reserved ½ cup of pasta water to the tomato sauce. Stir to combine and simmer for 5 minutes more. Add the pasta to the tomato sauce and stir to coat. Finally, add the torn basil leaves and serve.

FRIED TROUT

SERVES 6

Fried Trout is an amazingly tasty meal. I love this preparation because it's simple yet packed with flavor. My kids like it best made creekside, so I prepare ahead and bring everything in resealable bags.

2 pounds trout fillets

¾ cup coarsely ground cornmeal

1 teaspoon salt, plus extra for seasoning

½ teaspoon freshly ground black pepper, plus extra for seasoning

Zest from 1 lemon

Juice from 3 lemons

2 tablespoons ghee

¼ cup canola oil

2 teaspoons butter

Rinse the trout under cold water and pat dry as much as possible using paper towels. Mix the cornmeal with the salt and pepper and lemon zest. Season the dry trout with juice from one lemon and additional salt and pepper. Heat the ghee and canola oil in a large cast-iron skillet over medium heat.

Dredge the trout in the cornmeal and lay directly into the skillet, skin side up, for 5 to 6 minutes on the first side. Flip and cook for another 2 to 3 minutes on the skin side. When cooked, remove the fish from the pan and set the trout on a paper towel-lined plate. Drain the brown bits and oil from the pan and add the butter and remaining lemon juice. Season with salt and pepper to taste, then reduce the liquid by half. Place the fillets on a serving dish and pour the juice over them. Serve immediately.

BIRTHDAY MEATLOAF
SERVES 6 TO 8

Joe has never had much of a sweet tooth. When he says he wants dessert, he really means he just wants more of whatever he had for dinner. When we were first dating, my mom wanted to make Joe a birthday cake and asked him what kind he'd like best. He told her that he didn't really like cake but loved meatloaf. So now that's his tradition, meatloaf on his birthday, and if we do make a cake for him, we know it's really for us! Meatloaf is such a great dish. Not only is it healthy and high in protein, I'm always hiding vegetables in it. This meatloaf recipe is from my Aunt Cathy. She makes this when we visit, and there's never any left over.

2 ribs celery

2 carrots

8 cloves garlic

2 medium yellow onions

2½ teaspoons kosher salt

¾ teaspoon turmeric

¼ teaspoon cayenne

2 teaspoons chopped fresh thyme

1 tablespoon Worcestershire

2 tablespoons Dijon or brown mustard

1 tablespoon tomato paste

⅓ cup chicken or beef stock

1 egg, beaten

1 cup plain bread crumbs

3 pounds ground chuck (I know chuck is fattier, but it tastes better in a meatloaf.)

12 ounces ketchup (roughly one bottle)

Preheat the oven to 375°F. Rough chop the celery, carrots, garlic, and onion. Put the carrots in the food processor, and pulse 3 or 4 times (the carrots are usually tougher and need a couple more pulses than the other veggies). Add the onion, celery, and garlic and pulse the entire mixture again until finely chopped. In a large bowl, combine the pulsed vegetables with the salt, turmeric, cayenne, thyme, Worcestershire sauce, mustard, tomato paste, stock, and egg. Once these are well combined, add the ground meat and stir. Finally, add the breadcrumbs and be sure all are mixed together as evenly as possible. Form the meat into a loaf inside an 8 by 11-inch baking dish.

Next, top the meatloaf with the ketchup. I use roughly an entire bottle of ketchup to coat the top of the meatloaf. My kids love that part, and no one wants to get skimped and not get the pieces with baked ketchup on top. Use the back of a spoon to smooth the ketchup onto the meatloaf.

continued

Place the baking dish in your preheated oven and cook for 1½ to 2 hours. If you don't want your ketchup crust to split open, put a pan of water on the bottom rack below the meatloaf. The meatloaf will taste the same either way, but if you use the water pan, the ketchup crust will definitely look less cracked. Check to be sure that your meat thermometer reads 160°F at the thickest portion of the loaf before eating.

Note: This makes a large meatloaf, enough to feed 6 to 8 people. If that is more than you need, then consider freezing a portion of this. I like to halve the amount once the ingredients are all mixed together and put the portion to be frozen in the dish you plan to bake it in (I like the rectangular glass Pyrex because they have amazing lids and are so stackable in your freezer). I usually thaw out the frozen portion overnight in my refrigerator the day before baking, and then let it sit in my sink for a couple hours to be sure it's totally thawed.

GRILLED STEAK WITH MOONSHINE MARINADE

SERVES 4

This is a fantastic marinade for any steak, but our family typically does flank steak or New York strip. This is my daughter Maggie's absolute favorite, because she likes its sweet heat and especially loves the reduced sauce that goes on her sliced portions.

½ cup dark brown sugar

3 garlic cloves, minced small

½ cup Ole Smoky White Lightnin' Moonshine

⅓ cup soy sauce

1 tablespoon Dijon mustard

¼ teaspoon cayenne

1 teaspoon kosher salt

4 (6 to 8-ounce) steaks of your choice

Mix all the ingredients except the steak together in a bowl. Transfer the marinade to a large, plastic, resealable bag and add the steaks. Massage the steaks in the bag and marinate for at least 4 hours in the refrigerator.

Prepare a hot grill. Remove the steaks from the bag; transfer the marinade to a small stockpot. Bring the marinade to a boil and simmer until reduced by half. Cook the steaks for 3 to 4 minutes per side, or to your desired doneness. Once you slice your steak, drizzle the reduced marinade sauce on top.

TENNESSEE WHISKEY BURGER

SERVES 6

My family loves a good outdoor barbecue, and one of our favorite grillable meals is this Tennessee Whiskey Burger. It's packed with flavor! Not everyone in my family likes their burger with cheese, but these taste even better with a thick slice of sharp cheddar melted over them. Another tasty topping for this burger is Pimento Cheese (page 40).

2 pounds ground beef

2 tablespoons Ole Smoky Tennessee Straight Bourbon Whiskey

2 tablespoons Worcestershire sauce

½ teaspoon ground cumin

1 teaspoon ground oregano

1½ teaspoon garlic salt

½ teaspoon chili powder

1 teaspoon freshly ground pepper

Buns, lettuce, and tomato, for serving

Mix all the ingredients together well and form into 6 patties. Grill the burgers over medium-high heat for 5 to 6 minutes per side. Serve with grill-toasted buns, lettuce, and tomato.

CHAPTER NINE

SIDES

Well, do you know it's like I said
You better head back to Tennessee Jed
Tennessee, Tennessee, there ain't no place I'd rather be
Baby won't you carry me back to Tennessee

Tennessee Jed by Jerry Garcia & Robert Hunter

SAUTÉED SPINACH
SERVES 6

My husband is always asking for greens, and while these aren't collards, they are a healthy alternative. Sautéed Spinach is one of our family's favorite sides. I like it with a bit of turmeric, and the kids never seem to notice the difference! We eat this spinach at least once a week, sometimes with meatloaf and mashed potatoes, and other times with trout or chicken. It's very versatile!

Olive oil

1 pound fresh spinach

2 to 3 garlic cloves, minced

¼ teaspoon turmeric

½ teaspoon salt

¼ teaspoon freshly ground black pepper

Pour enough olive oil into a warmed heavy-bottomed Dutch oven to coat the bottom. Add the spinach, then cover it with the garlic, turmeric, salt, and pepper. Put the lid on the pan and cook on low for 4 to 5 minutes, or until spinach is half wilted. Remove from the heat and stir, then cover again for 2 minutes more. Serve immediately.

THE PERFECT PINTO BEANS
SERVES 8

Every Sunday while he was in law school, Joe's Aunt Claudia would make him a big pot of pinto beans to feed on for the week. With a side of onions, slaw, or chow-chow, beans and corn bread are always a hit. Pintos are relatively easy to make, and I always make sure my pot of them includes some sweet onion and bacon, which are the basis for their flavor.

1 (16-ounce) pound bag dried pinto beans

4 pieces bacon, whole

1 medium yellow onion, small diced

3 cloves of garlic, minced

1 bay leaf

1 teaspoon paprika

¼ teaspoon cayenne

1½ teaspoons kosher salt

Wash the beans well in a colander to remove any small stones or dirt. Be sure to pick over the dried beans and toss any that look funky. Soak the remaining beans in water overnight, or for 6 to 8 hours. Be sure your water level is an inch or two above the beans to give them plenty of moisture to absorb.

If you don't have time for soaking, you can parboil the beans by boiling them in water at a rapid boil for about 10 minutes. Drain the beans and follow the rest of the recipe as directed.

Place the drained beans, bacon, onion, garlic, and bay leaf into a large Dutch oven or soup pot. Add water to cover the beans by 1 inch and bring to a boil over medium-high heat. Lower the heat to medium-low and simmer for 1 hour.

Add the paprika, cayenne, and salt, and cook for another 1½ hours, or until the beans look creamy. Depending on how high your heat is, you may need to add more water, ½ cup at a time so you don't end up with beans that are too soupy, to be sure the beans finish cooking. Remove the bacon strips if you wish, or chop them up and mix them back into the beans. These beans will keep well in the refrigerator for 3 or 4 days.

CREAMY CHEESY GRITS
SERVES 8

At the family mill where our corn is milled for our moonshine mash, grits are a welcomed leftover. Grits are such an amazing comfort food and they're filling, too. I like to eat grits any time of day, with butter or cheese, however! The recipe below includes sharp cheddar cheese. If you are more of a purist, omit the cheese and the grits will still be fabulous. I like pairing these grits with the Pulled Pork and Apple Pie Moonshine (page 78), and sometimes I eat them for breakfast with the Candied Bacon (page 117).

1 cup stone-ground grits

1½ teaspoons salt

1 cup heavy cream

16 ounces shredded sharp cheddar cheese

¾ teaspoon freshly ground black pepper

Place the grits in a large bowl and cover with room temperature water. Give the grits a good stir and let sit for 5 minutes. Drain off the water and remove any excess floating corn or hulls.

In a medium or large stockpot, bring 3 cups of water to a boil. Add the rinsed grits and salt to the stockpot. Simmer over medium-high heat, uncovered, for 25 to 30 minutes. Add the heavy cream and simmer for 10 minutes more. Remove from the heat and fold in the shredded cheddar cheese and the pepper. Grits should be served hot. They don't keep in the pan for more than 1 or 2 hours.

FRIED POTATOES
SERVES 6 TO 8

Fried potatoes were a big part of my childhood. My parents had a garden and grew our own, so we ate these all the time. The key to great fried potatoes is soaking them in salted water for a few minutes before cooking, then drying them as well as possible before putting them in the pan. Fried potatoes pair well with almost any southern dish, but I especially like them with Moonshine Chicken (page 80) and Skillet-Fried Green Beans (page 107).

6 to 8 russet potatoes, peeled and sliced as uniformly as possibly, no more than ⅓-inch thick

Cold, salted water (I like to add 2 tablespoons of kosher salt for every 4 cups of water)

Cloth, for drying the potatoes

2 tablespoons ghee

Salt

Freshly ground black pepper

Put the sliced potatoes into the cold, salted water and let them soak for 10 minutes. Rinse them well, set them out on a clean dish towel, and cover them with another clean dish towel. Press to be sure the potatoes are as dry as possible or they won't cook correctly. Heat the ghee in a 12-inch cast-iron skillet. Lay the potatoes across. Do not overcrowd!

Fry 3 to 4 minutes per side, and season with salt and pepper to taste. You may have to cook them in batches. If this is the case, put the cooked potatoes on a paper towel-lined plate and set it in a warming drawer or low oven to keep them crispy.

SHINING SOUTHERN COLLARD GREENS

SERVES 8

A true southern meal is always accompanied by some greens. This recipe is my take on the classic and has some Ole Smoky White Lightnin' Moonshine to help these greens really shine. These greens make an appearance at our house quite often, and we always have them on New Year's Day.

2 medium sweet onions, small diced

8 cloves garlic, minced

4 slices thick cut bacon, cut into 1-inch squares

2 tablespoons honey

1 teaspoon whole mustard seeds

¾ teaspoon red pepper flakes

1½ teaspoons kosher salt

¼ teaspoon freshly ground black pepper

½ cup Ole Smoky White Lightnin' Moonshine

⅓ cup apple cider vinegar

4 cups chicken broth

3 bunches collard greens, stems cut off and leaves cut into 2-inch pieces

In a large stockpot over medium heat, sauté the onions, garlic, and bacon for 8 to 10 minutes, or until the onions are softened and nearly translucent. Add the honey, mustard seed, red pepper flakes, salt, and pepper and mix well. Next, add the Ole Smoky White Lightnin' Moonshine and cook for 5 minutes more.

Finally, add the vinegar, broth, and trimmed collard leaves. Give the mixture a good stir and bring to a boil. Decrease the heat to low, cover, and let simmer for nearly 2 hours, or until the collards are tender.

CREAMED CORN

SERVES 8

This is a southern staple. With crops of corn being abundant in the area, people can corn and then use it year-round in dishes like this one. I like to use the freshest corn possible to make this dish, so you can taste the summer, the sun, and the earth that went into that particular growing season. In a pinch, you can use 2 bags of frozen corn as a substitute.

3 tablespoons unsalted butter

10 ears corn, shucked and uncooked, kernels cut off the cob

1½ teaspoons kosher salt

1 tablespoon sugar

½ teaspoon freshly ground black pepper

1 tablespoon Ole Smoky Original Corn Moonshine

½ cup heavy cream

1½ cups whole milk

2 tablespoons flour

Heat a large cast-iron skillet or heavy-bottomed stockpot over medium heat and add the butter. Add the corn and panfry for 3 minutes. Next, add the salt, sugar, pepper, and corn whiskey. Panfry 3 to 5 minutes more.

Whisk together the cream, milk, and flour and pour into the pan. Cook and stir until the mixture is thickened. Remove from the heat, taste, and add more salt and pepper as desired. Serve piping hot!

HOMEMADE MASHED POTATOES
SERVES 8

Mashed potatoes are a must for Sunday dinner. They go with so many things, and there are so many ways of making them. Sometimes I like to throw in sour cream and parmesan, or sometimes I'm happy with butter and milk. Out of all the variations that we try, we always include lots of butter, salt, and freshly ground pepper. I hope you like these as much as we do!

4 pounds baking potatoes, such as russet (This is usually about 8 medium-sized potatoes, but I'd weigh them to be sure.)

2 cups heavy cream

4 tablespoons unsalted butter

2 teaspoons kosher salt

¾ teaspoon freshly ground black pepper

Peel and quarter the potatoes, place in a large stockpot, and cover with water. Boil the potatoes over medium-high heat until they can be cut easily with a butter knife, about 20 minutes.

In the meantime, warm the heavy cream and butter in a medium saucepan until the butter is melted.

Using a colander, drain water off the mashed potatoes and immediately put them back into the already hot stockpot. Add the warmed cream and butter. Using a hand potato masher or electric mixer, blend well, being careful not to overwork the potatoes. Season with salt and pepper to taste, stir again, and serve steaming hot.

SPIKED SOUTHERN APPLES
SERVES 6

Be sure you use a tart apple with this recipe. I prefer Granny Smith, and I prefer to peel them before slicing. I add some of our moonshine to these for extra flavor, but they are great with or without it. I use Ole Smoky Apple Pie Moonshine because it already has cinnamon and allspice in it. I like serving these apples alongside my Moonshine Chicken (page 80) or Pork Chops and Gravy (page 79). They are also great with pulled pork, and can even stand alone as a dessert topping for vanilla ice cream. They are a very versatile item!!

4 teaspoons unsalted butter

5 Granny Smith apples, cored, peeled and cut into ¼ -inch slices

Juice from ½ lemon

¼ cup granulated sugar

1 tablespoon Ole Smoky Apple Pie Moonshine

¼ cup dark brown sugar

¾ teaspoon ground cinnamon

Heat a large skillet over medium heat and melt the butter. Add the apples to the skillet, along with lemon juice, granulated sugar, and apple pie moonshine, and stir to combine. Simmer the apples until the butter is absorbed, but be careful NOT to overcook.

Add the brown sugar and toss to combine. Lower the heat and let the apples cook until the sugar is dissolved. Turn off the heat and sprinkle the cinnamon over the apples, then toss to combine. Serve warm.

SUMMER SQUASH CASSEROLE
SERVES 8

Squash casserole is a popular dish as well as a great way to use large amounts of garden squash and herbs. People love this particular recipe, and I think it's because we go the extra mile with the breadcrumbs by adding some garlic, fresh herbs, and butter. This dish travels well and is always welcome at a neighborhood potluck or summer barbecue.

1 cup yellow onion, small diced

2 tablespoons ghee

¼ cup olive oil

8 cups yellow squash, coarsely chopped

4 cups zucchini squash, coarsely chopped

16 ounces chicken broth

¾ teaspoon kosher salt

½ teaspoon fresh ground black pepper

½ cup sour cream

16 ounces freshly grated sharp cheddar cheese

2 eggs, beaten

1 (14-ounce) box (4 sleeves) Ritz crackers, crushed by hand either in sleeve or in a bowl

2 cloves garlic, minced

½ cup butter, melted

1 teaspoon minced fresh thyme

1 teaspoon minced fresh basil

Preheat the oven to 375°F. In a large Dutch oven, sauté the onion in ghee and olive oil over medium heat until soft and translucent, 6 to 8 minutes. Add the squashes and chicken broth and simmer until all are soft, about 10 minutes.

Use a handheld potato masher to mash the squash, and be sure all the onions are mixed together well. Drain the liquid off the squash (I use a spaghetti strainer for this; a little liquid left is okay), pour into a large bowl, and let cool for 15 minutes.

Add the salt and pepper, sour cream, cheese, and beaten eggs to the squash. Mix well.

In a separate large bowl, mix the crushed crackers with the garlic, most of the melted butter (reserve 2 tablespoons for the topping), and fresh herbs. Take a little over half of the cracker mixture and add it to the squash mixture. Transfer the squash mixture to a 9 by 13-inch baking dish and top with remaining cracker mixture. Drizzle the remaining 2 tablespoons of melted butter over the top. Cover with aluminum foil and bake for 40 minutes. Uncover and bake 10 minutes more, until golden brown and bubbly.

SKILLET-FRIED GREEN BEANS

SERVES 8

I love to skillet fry my green beans much the same way I do apples, with a little butter. This manner of cooking is best with really fresh beans, and you still have a crunchy, lovely veggie at the end.

2 pounds fresh green beans, strings removed and ends trimmed

3 cloves garlic, minced

2 tablespoons ghee or butter

½ teaspoon salt

½ teaspoon freshly ground black pepper

Juice from ½ lemon

In a large cast-iron skillet, sauté the green beans and garlic in ghee or butter until they have an al dente type of tender crispness, about 5 minutes. Season with salt and pepper, and finish with the lemon juice. Serve immediately.

TOMATO PIE
SERVES 6

If you've ever wondered what to do with all of those fresh tomatoes in your summer garden, look no further than this delectable tomato pie. This is a crowd-pleaser and travels well to family dinner or neighborhood potlucks. I'd consider making double of this dish—it gets eaten first and fast!!

1 (8-inch) unbaked pie shell, (from scratch, or frozen)

4 heirloom tomatoes

1 teaspoon kosher salt

4 ounces gruyere, shredded

4 ounces fontina, shredded

2 ounces parmesan, shredded

½ cup mayonnaise

¼ teaspoon cayenne

½ teaspoon freshly ground black pepper

½ medium yellow onion, small diced

½ cup basil (about 16 leaves), chiffonade

continued

Preheat the oven to 350°F. Prepare your pie crust with pie weights and prebake for roughly 10 minutes, until golden brown.

While the crust is baking, prepare your tomatoes. Cut each tomato in half and squeeze like an orange to get the first round of juice out. After this, coarsely chop the tomatoes; you need roughly 3 cups of chopped tomatoes. Season the tomatoes with salt and place them in a colander over a bowl to drain for at least 10 minutes.

Then, try again to get as much moisture out of the tomatoes as possible. You can squeeze them again using a dish towel, or even paper towels. This step is really important, as you don't want a soggy pie bottom. Seriously squeeze the juice out of these tomatoes.

While the pie crust is cooling, mix the shredded cheeses, mayonnaise, cayenne, and pepper together in a small bowl. Now layer the pie. Start by putting the onions on the bottom, then add the drained tomatoes and chopped basil. Next, add the cheese mixture and smooth it out. Put the tomato pie in the oven and bake for 30 to 40 minutes, until golden brown on top and bubbly on the sides.

CHAPTER TEN

BRUNCH

Back where I come from
I'm an old Tennessean
And I'm proud as anyone
That's where I come from

Back Where I Come From by Mac McAnally

HANGOVER FRENCH TOAST

SERVES 4

While recipe testing for this book, I enlisted the help of a good friend and one of the original members of the Ole Smoky team. She made this recipe its original way, with regular whipped cream and maple syrup, then convinced me that if people are going to eat moonshine-spiked French toast, they'll want moonshine in the toppings, too! So, these toppings are her creation. Thanks, Jill!!

3 eggs

½ teaspoon ground cinnamon

1 tablespoon sugar

½ cup Ole Smoky Mountain Java

Butter, for greasing the pan

8 slices thick white bread (challah, brioche, or even a French baguette will work)

Fully Loaded Maple Syrup (page 115)

Spiked Whipped Cream, for serving (page 114)

Beat the eggs, sugar, and cinnamon in a medium bowl. Add the Ole Smoky Mountain Java and beat again. Over medium heat, melt enough butter in a 12-inch skillet or cast-iron pan to coat the bottom. Dip the bread slices in the egg and moonshine mixture to generously coat, but let any extra drip back in the bowl. Fry on one side for 3 minutes, until golden brown. Flip to cook the other side for another 5 minutes, until golden brown. Serve with the Fully Loaded Maple Syrup and Spiked Whipped Cream.

SPIKED WHIPPED CREAM

SERVES 4

This is excellent on French toast and also as a topping on coffee, hot cocoa, or ice cream. My family calls it Christmas Cream because of the cinnamon and nutmeg! Whatever you call it, it tastes REALLY good!

½ cup heavy whipping cream, as cold as possible

1½ teaspoons sugar

2 tablespoons Ole Smoky Mountain Java

⅛ teaspoon cinnamon

Pinch of freshly grated nutmeg

In a medium chilled bowl, combine the heavy whipping cream and sugar. Whip until stiff peaks form, about 8 minutes. Add the Ole Smoky Mountain Java, cinnamon, and nutmeg. Whip again until just combined. Serve immediately.

FULLY LOADED MAPLE SYRUP

MAKES 1 CUP

Serve over pancakes, waffles, or French toast. Or try dipping bacon and sausage in it. The opportunities are endless with this scrumptious syrup.

1 cup maple syrup

3 tablespoons Ole Smoky Salty Caramel Whiskey

In a small bowl, mix the Ole Smoky Salty Caramel Whiskey with the maple syrup. This stores well in an airtight container in a refrigerator for up to 1 week.

CANDIED BACON
SERVES 2 TO 4

Do you want to try something that is SO extra? Skillet-fried bacon is definitely my favorite version of bacon, but try adding some brown sugar, cayenne, and moonshine for a whole other level of bacon goodness.

1 cup packed dark brown sugar

4 tablespoons Ole Smoky White Lightnin' Moonshine

4 tablespoons maple syrup

Black pepper

¼ teaspoon cayenne (optional)

1 pound thick-cut bacon

Preheat oven to 350°F. Line a baking pan with foil and put a cooling rack over it. (The foil helps with clean up!) Mix the brown sugar, Ole Smoky White Lightnin' Moonshine, maple syrup, black pepper, and cayenne, if using, in a shallow bowl. Dredge each bacon slice on both sides through the sugar mixture.

Place the bacon on the rack and bake for 25 to 35 minutes, depending on the thickness of your bacon, until it's browned and crisp. For extra flavor, pull the bacon out at about 20 minutes and baste it with the remaining sugar mixture. Return to the oven for the remaining 5 to 15 minutes of cooking time and serve while hot.

BISCUITS & GRAVY
SERVES 4

A good sausage gravy recipe is essential to a southern cook. I have no idea why, but gravy made in a home kitchen always tastes far superior to anything I can find in a restaurant. Maybe it's the quantities we cook in, or maybe it's because we usually eat directly off the stove in my house, but it just tastes better. Use the Buttermilk Biscuit recipe (page 44) from the Southern Breads chapter. Also, it's imperative that you listen to "Biscuits" by Kacey Musgraves while making these. It truly makes the process more fun.

1 pound pork breakfast sausage

2 tablespoons unsalted butter

¼ cup all-purpose flour

3 cups whole milk

½ teaspoon salt

½ teaspoon freshly ground pepper

4 Buttermilk Biscuits (page 44)

In a large skillet, cook the sausage over medium-high heat for about 10 minutes, using a wooden spoon or spatula to continue breaking it up so it crumbles. Once browned, check the oil content of the meat. Drain off all except about 1 tablespoon of the sausage grease. Add the butter and stir until melted.

Next, sprinkle the flour uniformly over the pan and stir, allowing the flour to cook with the fats for 3 to 4 minutes. Finally, add the milk and stir continuously over medium heat until it thickens, usually 6 to 10 minutes. Season with salt and pepper to taste and serve immediately with the biscuits.

HASH BROWN CASSEROLE WITH BUTTERED CORNFLAKES

SERVES 8

This casserole is great for a crowd, whether served at brunch or alongside some fried chicken at dinner. I often take this to neighborhood potlucks, and there's never a spoonful left over. It's also especially popular among teenage boys like my son, Joseph, and his friends.

Hash Browns

- ½ cup unsalted butter, plus more for greasing pan
- 2-pound bag frozen shredded hash browns, thawed
- 1 small yellow onion, small diced
- 2 tablespoons ghee
- ¼ cup all-purpose flour
- 2 cups whole milk
- 2 cups shredded cheddar cheese (fresh grated tastes best)
- 1 (1-ounce) container sour cream
- 1 teaspoon kosher salt
- ½ teaspoon freshly ground black pepper

Topping

- ¼ cup (½ stick) butter
- 2 cups cornflakes

To make the hash browns, preheat the oven to 350°F. Grease a 9 by 13-inch casserole dish with butter. In a large stockpot, sauté the onion in the ghee until translucent, 5 to 6 minutes. Turn off the heat, add the hash browns, and stir together until well coated.

Meanwhile, in a separate large saucepan, heat ½ cup butter and sprinkle flour into the pan, whisking constantly while the flour "cooks" for about 2 minutes. Slowly pour in the 2 cups of whole milk and stir until thickened. Add the cheddar cheese and combine, then remove from the heat and add the sour cream, salt, and pepper.

Add the milk and cheese mixture to the hash browns. Stir well to be sure all are coated. Pour the entire mixture into your prepared casserole dish.

To make the cornflake topping, melt the butter in a small saucepan. Toss the melted butter with the cornflakes in a flat dish. Sprinkle over the casserole and bake for 45 to 55 minutes, or until golden brown and bubbly.

RAMPS & EGGS
SERVES 2 TO 4

The Ramp Festival in Cosby, Tennessee, was a locally famous festival during my childhood (unfortunately they stopped having it ten years ago). We always looked forward to the first Sunday in May, because the celebration of ramps (wild mountain onions) meant great food, music, games, crafts, and even a beauty pageant. Young women from the area vied to be named Maid of Ramps and attendees ranged from President Truman to Tennessee Ernie Ford. Makeshift stoves on the farm were used to serve this breakfast dish all day, and it was always accompanied by a Skillet-Fried Cornpones (page 47). This dish also pairs well with a Moonshine Bloody Mary (page 31) or Beer Shinearita (page 27).

2 tablespoons ghee

8 to 12 ramps, washed, dried, and ends trimmed

4 large eggs

¼ teaspoon salt

¼ teaspoon freshly ground black pepper

Heat a large cast-iron skillet over medium heat and add the ghee. When the ghee is hot, make sure it covers the entire skillet and add the ramps. After about 1 minute, move the ramps over to one side of the skillet.

On the other side of the skillet, crack the eggs into the pan and cook sunny side up for a few minutes. Flip, if that's your preference. Sprinkle the eggs with salt and pepper, and serve immediately.

CHAPTER ELEVEN

DESSERTS

You're as smooth as Tennessee whiskey
You're as sweet as strawberry wine
You're as warm as a glass of brandy
And honey, I stay stoned on your love all the time

Tennessee Whiskey by Linda Hargrove & Dean Dillon

WHISKEY BUTTER FUDGE
MAKES 12 TO 16 SMALL SQUARES

Ole Smoky Candy Kitchen was opened in 1950 by my grandparents, Dave and Peggy Dych. Since then, millions of visitors to Gatlinburg have stopped to watch taffy and fudge being made in the window. Candymakers, dressed in crisp white uniforms, stir enormous copper kettles. While our candy shop sells everything from chocolates to caramel apples, fudge is one of our most popular items. My grandmother's fudge is delicious because it's homemade from scratch. We've never used a mix, and never will, because it's impossible to get that same great flavor. The recipe that follows here is similar to what we do at the Candy Kitchen, with some added Ole Smoky Whiskey.

4 tablespoons unsalted butter, plus extra for the pan

3 cups sugar

⅔ cups unsweetened cocoa powder

¼ cup Ole Smoky Salty Caramel Whiskey

½ teaspoon salt

1¼ cups half-and-half

1 teaspoon vanilla extract

Line an 8-inch square pan with parchment paper. Butter/grease the upper side of the parchment. In a heavy-bottomed, medium stockpot, combine the sugar, cocoa powder, Ole Smoky Salty Caramel Whiskey, and salt, and stir with a wooden spoon. Add the half-and-half and stir again.

Using medium heat instead of high, cook until the mixture boils, stirring continuously the entire time. Turn the heat down to low and cook without disturbing (no stirring!) until 234°F is reached on your candy thermometer.

Remove the pot from the heat and add 4 tablespoons of butter and the vanilla. Resist the urge to stir this! Leave it alone until the candy thermometer reads about 110°F, then stir vigorously for about 5 minutes, until the mixture loses a bit of its shiny, glossy look. Pour this quickly into the prepared pan and let it cool. Cut into squares and store in an airtight container for 1 to 2 weeks.

APPALACHIAN APPLE STACK CAKE

SERVES 10

An Appalachian standard and favorite, stack cake is laborious, but worth the effort. This cake is the prize of every cake walk and fairground competition. It is the very best version of Apple Stack Cake, and since I rarely see it outside of the south, I'm so happy to share it with you and give it its due. And of course, I've added a special Ole Smoky Salty Caramel Whiskey topping (page 126) that is worth the extra effort!

Cake

4½ cups all-purpose flour

1½ teaspoons salt

½ teaspoon baking soda

1½ teaspoons baking powder

½ teaspoon ground cinnamon

1 cup (2 sticks) unsalted butter, room temperature

1½ cups granulated sugar

1 cup molasses

2 eggs

½ cup buttermilk

Apple Filling

32 ounces (2 pounds) dried apples

2 cups granulated sugar

2 cups dark brown sugar

3 teaspoons ground cinnamon

2 teaspoons nutmeg

1 teaspoon allspice

3 tablespoons molasses

½ cup Ole Smoky Apple Pie Moonshine

¼ cup Ole Smoky Salty Caramel Whiskey

2½ cups water

To make the cake, preheat the oven to 350°F. Cut 6 pieces of parchment paper the size of an 8 or 9-inch circular cake pan. Set aside.

Place the flour, salt, baking soda, baking powder, and cinnamon in a medium bowl and whisk to combine. Set aside.

In a stand mixer fitted with the paddle attachment, cream the butter and sugar together. Add the molasses and mix well. Scrape down the sides of the bowl with a rubber spatula to ensure all the ingredients are combining together. Add the eggs, one at a time, on low speed, mixing well and continuing to stop and scrape the sides with the rubber spatula.

Add the buttermilk and the dry ingredients about a third at a time. Continue stopping the mixer and scraping the sides of the bowl until all are incorporated. The dough should be thick. Turn the dough out on a floured surface and mold it into a disc. Wrap in plastic wrap and refrigerate for one hour.

Set your 6 circular pieces of parchment paper out separately onto a flat work surface. Divide the dough into 6 equal parts and set on each of the 6 circles of parchment. Roll the dough out to fit the circle as well as possible. You can always roll over the circle and come back and cut off the excess portion. The goal is to get circles of dough as close as possible to the 9-inch cake pan size, so they'll be easy to stack.

With the parchment paper left underneath the circles, bake them on cookie sheets for about 10 minutes, or until a toothpick inserted in the center comes out clean. Remove the cakes from the baking sheets to cool on wire racks.

To make the apple filling, combine all the filling ingredients in a large stockpot and simmer over low heat for 4 to 5 minutes. Turn off the heat and let cool for 5 minutes. Using a rubber spatula, transfer this mixture to a blender or the bowl of a food processor. Pulse until combined.

To assemble the cake, place 1 cake layer onto a plate and top with roughly 1 cup of the apple filling. Repeat with the remaining cake layers; don't put filling on the very top of the cake. Put waxed paper over the top layer, then wrap the entire cake in plastic wrap. Put in a refrigerator overnight, so that the filling gets to soak into the cake. Serve with Creamy Salty Caramel Sauce (page 126).

CREAMY SALTY CARAMEL SAUCE

MAKES 3 CUPS

Many of you can probably relate to my sincere love of icings and toppings. I used to use whipped cream for an additional topping for apple stack cake, but I've since changed over to this lovely, creamy sauce. It adds layers of complementary flavors. This sauce is also excellent spooned over fresh berries.

2 cups heavy cream

1½ cups sugar, divided

1 teaspoon vanilla extract

Pinch of freshly grated nutmeg

8 egg yolks

3 tablespoons Ole Smoky Salty Caramel Whiskey

Place the cream, ¾ cup sugar, vanilla, and nutmeg in a medium saucepan over medium heat. Mix well and heat until it starts to boil. In a bowl, whisk the egg yolks and remaining ¾ cup sugar until well combined. Slowly whisk the simmering cream into the egg mixture, 1 tablespoon at a time, and mix well. Slowly add the rest of the hot mixture, continuing to whisk. If you add the hot liquid too quickly, you'll end up with scrambled eggs.

Transfer the mixture to a double boiler for 8 to 12 minutes, stirring constantly. Pass through a strainer and cool over an ice bath. Finally, mix in the Ole Smoky Salty Caramel Whiskey. Refrigerate until ready to use, for up to 5 or 6 days. Spoon half the sauce over the apple stack cake and reserve half the sauce to spoon over each piece as it's served.

CHOCOLATE-COVERED MOONSHINE CHERRIES

MAKES ROUGHLY 30 TO 40 CHERRIES, DEPENDING ON SIZE

These are, quite literally, the cherry bomb of desserts. They are a bit arduous to make but absolutely worth it. You will definitely be praised and lauded if you bring these to your next dinner party. You can add a white chocolate drizzle or pinch of sea salt as a final step to enhance the flavors to your personal preference.

Cherries

2 (13.5 ounce) jars stemmed maraschino cherries, drained

1 (750 ml) jar Ole Smoky White Lightnin' Moonshine

Filling

3 cups sifted confectioners' sugar

¼ cup unsalted butter, melted

¼ cup sweetened condensed milk

2 tablespoons Ole Smoky Mountain Java

½ teaspoon salt

Chocolate Coating

12 to 16 ounces semisweet chocolate of your choice

To prepare the cherries, place the strained maraschino cherries into an empty 16-ounce mason jar. Add enough Ole Smoky White Lightnin' Moonshine to cover the cherries completely. Leave for at least 24 hours to allow the cherries to absorb the moonshine.

Strain the moonshine cherries out of the White Lightnin'. Reserve the cherry-flavored moonshine for another use. Place the moonshine cherries on a kitchen towel and lightly wipe them off so they aren't too wet. Transfer the cherries to a baking sheet lined with wax paper and freeze them for 1 to 2 hours.

To make the filling, combine the confectioners' sugar, melted butter, condensed milk, Ole Smoky Mountain Java, and salt in a medium bowl. Put this mixture in the refrigerator until firm, about 20 minutes or so.

continued

Remove the filling from the refrigerator and coat the cherries with it by forming a ball around the cherry with the white filling. I like to keep a little bowl of confectioners' sugar off to the side and use it on my hands and fingers while putting the filling around the cherries. The filling is super sticky and the confectioners' sugar can be a lifesaver. Once finished coating them all, return the cherries on the wax paper-lined baking sheet to the freezer for 1 to 2 hours.

To make the chocolate coating, melt the chocolate in either a double boiler or the microwave and dip the cherries in the melted chocolate, being sure to get the chocolate well up on the stem. Set them back on the wax paper, and refrigerate until set and firm. Be careful with these cherries—they'll bite you back!

WILD BLACKBERRY COBBLER
SERVES 4

Blackberry cobbler is one of those quintessential desserts that everyone has tried at least once. You can serve it with whipped cream, but we prefer vanilla ice cream. The sweet, cold vanilla ice cream melts against the hot blackberries and makes something truly special. You can enjoy this any time of year with frozen blackberries, but it's especially tasty in the summer with fresh wild berries.

5 tablespoons butter, melted, plus extra for the pan

4 cups freshly picked blackberries

Juice from one lemon

2 tablespoons Ole Smoky Blackberry Moonshine

1 cup plus 2 tablespoons sugar, divided

1 large egg, lightly beaten

1 cup all-purpose flour

Ground cinnamon, for serving

Vanilla ice cream, for serving

Preheat the oven to 375°F. Grease an 8-inch square dish with butter. Wash and dry the blackberries, then place them into the greased dish. Sprinkle the lemon juice, Ole Smoky Blackberry Moonshine, and 2 tablespoons of sugar over the berries.

Mix together the egg, remaining 1 cup of sugar, 5 tablespoons melted butter, and flour in a medium bowl. Spoon this as evenly as possible over the fruit. Bake for 40 to 50 minutes, or until lightly browned and bubbly. Sprinkle the top with cinnamon and add a hefty scoop of vanilla ice cream to each serving.

SPIKED BANANA PUDDING
SERVES 4 TO 6

This is the banana pudding of Fourth of July picnics, family gatherings, and many a southern childhood. Easy to make and easy to love, I hope this tastes like a happy scoopful of nostalgia, and floods your taste buds with memories.

¾ cup sugar, divided

¼ cup all-purpose flour

½ teaspoon salt

1 teaspoon vanilla extract

3 cups whole milk

4 large eggs

2 tablespoons Ole Smoky Tennessee Straight Bourbon Whiskey

5 to 6 Bananas

1 (11-ounce) box vanilla wafers (You'll use most of the bag but have a few left over.)

Preheat the oven to 425°F. In a medium saucepan over medium-high heat, whisk together ½ cup of sugar, flour, salt, vanilla extract, and whole milk. Cook, stirring constantly using a whisk, until the mixture gets thick and bubbly, 8 to 10 minutes. If you don't whisk constantly, the bottom will brown. Decrease the heat to low and stir for a couple more minutes. Remove from the heat.

Using two bowls, separate 3 of the 4 eggs into yolks and whites. Add a pinch of salt to the egg whites and set aside. Add the fourth egg in its entirety to the yolks. Add a tablespoon of the hot pudding to the yolks and stir well. Add another tablespoon and repeat. Slowly add the entire yolk mixture back to the saucepan along with the whiskey. Stir over medium heat for 2 minutes, then remove from the heat and set aside.

Cut the bananas into ½ thick slices. In an 8-inch square pan, first make a layer of wafers, followed by a layer of bananas on top, and repeat. You will use all of the bananas and most of the wafers. Pour the pudding over the top of the layers, starting with the edges first, and then moving into the middle until completely covered.

To make the meringue, beat the reserved egg whites until stiff peaks form. Beat in the remaining ¼ cup of sugar until combined. Put the egg whites on top of the pudding and bake for 5 to 8 minutes, until lightly browned on top. Serve warm.

COUNTRY CROSTATA WITH STRAWBERRIES & BLUE FLAME

Crostata is sort of like an upside-down pie in freeform. You still roll out the pie dough and fill it, but then fold up the edges around your fruit. I like serving mine with whipped cream blended with our famous Ole Smoky Tennessee Mud.

Dough

- 1¼ cups all-purpose flour
- 2 tablespoons sugar
- ½ teaspoon kosher salt
- ½ cup (1 stick) unsalted butter, cold, cubed (Keep this in the fridge until the last minute to keep it as cold as possible.)
- 4 tablespoons ice water, as cold as possible without it being ice

Filling

- 2 tablespoons unsalted butter
- 3 stalks rhubarb, sliced into ½-inch pieces
- ½ cup sugar
- 1 teaspoon finely grated lemon zest
- 2 tablespoons cornstarch
- 3 tablespoons Ole Smoky Blue Flame Moonshine
- 2 cups strawberries, hulled and quartered

For the dough, use a food processor to pulse the flour, sugar, and salt together until well combined. Add the butter and pulse until it looks like frozen peas. Add the water all together, and pulse just a few times until the dough sticks together. Turn the dough out onto a floured surface and form into a disc. Wrap in plastic wrap and refrigerate for at least 1 hour before use.

For the filling, melt the butter in a skillet over medium heat and sauté the rhubarb until softened but not falling apart, 6 to 8 minutes. Mix in the sugar and continue cooking until it dissolves. Mix in the lemon zest, sprinkle on the cornstarch, add the Blue Flame, and stir. Bring to a simmer for 2 minutes. Remove from heat and fold in the strawberries. Let cool.

Preheat the oven to 400°F. Turn the chilled dough out onto a lightly floured surface and roll it into a large circle, 10 to 12 inches in diameter. I like to use parchment paper both on the countertop surface and on top of the dough to make it easier to roll it out. Add the fruit mixture and fold the dough up around the sides of the fruit, using the parchment paper underneath to aid you in folding. Bake for 40 minutes, or until golden brown and bubbly.

TENNESSEE MUD WHIPPED CREAM

SERVES 6

If you ever thought whipped cream was decadent, then this is really going to blow your mind. Creamier, boozier, and sweeter, it's the only whipped topping you'll ever want to eat!

1¼ cups heavy whipping cream, very cold

2 tablespoons confectioners' sugar

2 tablespoons Ole Smoky Tennessee Mud

In a medium bowl, combine the heavy whipping cream and confectioners' sugar. Whip until stiff peaks form. Add the Ole Smoky Tennessee Mud and whip again until combined. Serve immediately!

WHISKEY PECAN PIE
SERVES 6

My grandmother made the best pecan pie I've ever tasted. Here's a little riff on her recipe with some Ole Smoky Tennessee Straight Bourbon Whiskey added into it. Being that my grandmother NEVER missed her five o'clock cocktail and often gave us grandchildren schnapps before bed to settle us down, I know she would approve.

3 eggs, lightly beaten

½ cup light brown sugar

½ cup light corn syrup

½ cup dark corn syrup

1 teaspoon vanilla extract

½ teaspoon kosher salt

⅓ cup unsalted butter, melted

2 tablespoons Ole Smoky Tennessee Straight Bourbon Whiskey

1 (9-inch) pre-made pie shell

2 cups pecans, coarsely chopped

Preheat the oven to 375°F. Mix the beaten eggs together with the sugar and corn syrups, vanilla, salt, melted butter, and Ole Smoky Tennessee Straight Bourbon Whiskey in a medium bowl.

Using a fork, prick the sides and bottom of the pie shell every inch or so. Spread the pecans out evenly in the pie shell, and then pour the liquid mixture over them. Bake for 40 minutes, until set around the edges and a little jiggly in the center. It will continue cooking as it cools.

At age 92, Peggy Dych still went to work daily. Here she is in her office at Ole Smoky Candy Kitchen.

HOMEMADE OATMEAL CREAM PIES

MAKES ROUGHLY 20 SANDWICHED COOKIES

This is an old-fashioned dessert with a wholesomely delicious approach. As good as it tastes, it's tough to eat more than one. Make room, though, as these are as amazing as they are rich.

1 pound butter (4 sticks), room temperature

1 cup granulated sugar

3 cups light brown sugar

4 large eggs

1 tablespoon plus 1 teaspoon vanilla

3½ cups all-purpose flour

1½ teaspoons kosher salt

1 tablespoon baking soda

1¼ teaspoons ground cinnamon

1 pound oats (about half of a large oatmeal tin)

Apple Pie Moonshine Buttercream (page 139)

Preheat the oven to 375°F. In a stand mixer fitted with the paddle attachment, cream the butter and sugars until light and fluffy. With the mixer on medium speed, add the eggs and vanilla and beat.

Sift together the flour, salt, baking soda, and cinnamon in a separate mixing bowl. Beating on low speed, gradually add the flour mixture to the butter mixture and mix until thoroughly combined. Scrape down the sides of the bowl if necessary. Add the oats. Mix 5 to 10 seconds to evenly incorporate. Refrigerate the dough for 30 minutes before moving on to the next step. On a cookie sheet lined with parchment paper, put ping-pong-ball-sized cookies about 2 inches apart. Bake for 10 minutes. Once cooled, spread the cookies with Apple Pie Moonshine Buttercream. Store in an airtight container in your refrigerator for up to 5 days.

APPLE PIE MOONSHINE BUTTERCREAM

Homemade buttercream icing mixed with Ole Smoky Apple Pie Moonshine is such a perfect combination that I would put it on almost any dessert: over pumpkin bread, on top of carrot cake, and especially in between two homemade oatmeal cookies. This recipe makes a lot of icing (the oatmeal cookie recipe makes a lot of cookies, so you'll likely use it all). However, if you are making it for a two-layer cake, you may want to cut the recipe in half. If you want to save some icing for next week's pumpkin bread, it will keep well in the freezer folded up in plastic wrap for a couple weeks. Or maybe it's just me, but you can also happily sit like a kid on the kitchen floor and finish a bowl of icing like I do!

3 cups (6 sticks) unsalted butter, room temperature

1 pound confectioners' sugar

½ tablespoon vanilla extract

¼ teaspoon salt

2 tablespoons 70 proof Ole Smoky Apple Pie Moonshine

Cream the butter and sugar together in a large bowl until light and fluffy and the butter has nearly doubled in size, 3 to 5 minutes, depending on the speed of your mixer. Gently stir in the vanilla, salt, and moonshine until combined.

MAMAW BAKER'S PECAN SANDIES

MAKES ABOUT 3 DOZEN COOKIES

Joe's Mamaw Baker made these cookies regularly and always had them sitting in a metal tin for visitors. I'm trying to continue that tradition, but my family keeps gobbling them up before any visitors ever arrive.

1 cup (2 sticks) butter, room temperature

⅓ cup granulated sugar

2 teaspoons water

2 teaspoons vanilla

2 cups all-purpose flour, sifted

1 cup chopped pecans

Confectioners' sugar

In a stand mixer fitted with the paddle attachment, cream the butter and sugar together until well combined. Scrape down the sides of the bowl, then add the water and vanilla, and mix well. Scrape down the sides of the bowl again. Slowly add the flour and nuts while mixing on low, being careful not to overwork the dough. Scrape down the sides of the bowl and chill the dough for at least 4 hours.

Preheat the oven to 325°F. Shape the chilled dough into 1-inch balls and bake on an ungreased cookie sheet for about 20 minutes. Remove from the pan and cool until room temperature. Roll the baked cookies in confectioners' sugar. Store these at room temperature in an airtight container for up to 5 days, if they last that long!

METRIC CONVERSIONS AND EQUIVALENTS

To Convert	Multiply
Ounces to grams	Ounces by 28.35
Pounds to kilograms	Pounds by.454
Teaspoons to milliliters	Teaspoons by 4.93
Tablespoons to milliliters	Tablespoons by 14.79
Fluid ounces to milliliters	Fluid ounces by 29.57
Cups to milliliters	Cups by 240
Cups to liters	Cups by .236
Pints to liters	Pints by .473
Quarts to liters	Quarts by .946
Gallons to liters	Gallons by 3.785
Inches to centimeters	Inches by 2.54

Oven Temperatures

To convert Fahrenheit to Celsius, subtract 32 from Fahrenheit, multiply the result by 5, then divide by 9.

Description	Fahrenheit	Celsius	British Gas Mark
Very cool	200°	95°	0
Very cool	225°	110°	¼
Very cool	250°	120°	½
Cool	275°	135°	1
Cool	300°	150°	2
Warm	325°	165°	3
Moderate	350°	175°	4
Moderately hot	375°	190°	5
Fairly hot	400°	200°	6
Hot	425°	220°	7
Very hot	450°	230°	8
Very hot	475°	245°	9

Common Ingredients and Their Approximate Equivalents

1 cup uncooked white rice = 185 grams
1 cup all-purpose flour = 120 grams
1 stick butter (4 ounces • ½ cup • 8 tablespoons) = 110 grams
1 cup butter (8 ounces • 2 sticks • 16 tablespoons) = 220 grams
1 cup brown sugar, firmly packed = 213 grams
1 cup granulated sugar = 200 grams

Information compiled from a variety of sources, including *Recipes into Type* by Joan Whitman and Dolores Simon (Newton, MA: Biscuit Books, 1993); *The New Food Lover's Companion* by Sharon Tyler Herbst (Hauppauge, NY: Barron's, 2013); and *Rosemary Brown's Big Kitchen Instruction Book* (Kansas City, MO: Andrews McMeel, 1998).

Approximate Metric Equivalents

Volume

¼ teaspoon	1 milliliter
½ teaspoon	2.5 milliliters
¾ teaspoon	4 milliliters
1 teaspoon	5 milliliters
1¼ teaspoons	6 milliliters
1½ teaspoons	7.5 milliliters
1¾ teaspoons	8.5 milliliters
2 teaspoons	10 milliliters
1 tablespoon (½ fluid ounce)	15 milliliters
2 tablespoons (1 fluid ounce)	30 milliliters
¼ cup	60 milliliters
⅓ cup	80 milliliters
½ cup (4 fluid ounces)	120 milliliters
⅔ cup	160 milliliters
¾ cup	180 milliliters
1 cup (8 fluid ounces)	240 milliliters
1¼ cups	300 milliliters
1½ cups (12 fluid ounces)	360 milliliters
1⅔ cups	400 milliliters
2 cups (1 pint)	480 milliliters
3 cups	720 milliliters
4 cups (1 quart)	0.96 liter
1 quart plus ¼ cup	1 liter
4 quarts (1 gallon)	3.8 liters

Mass

¼ ounce	7 grams
½ ounce	14 grams
¾ ounce	21 grams
1 ounce	28 grams
1¼ ounces	35 grams
1½ ounces	42.5 grams
1⅔ ounces	47 grams
2 ounces	57 grams
3 ounces	85 grams
4 ounces (¼ pound)	113 grams
5 ounces	142 grams
6 ounces	170 grams
7 ounces	198 grams
8 ounces (½ pound)	227 grams
16 ounces (1 pound)	454 grams
35.25 ounces (2.2 pounds)	1 kilogram

Length

⅛ inch	3 millimeters
¼ inch	6.25 millimeters
½ inch	1.25 centimeters
1 inch	2.5 centimeters
2 inches	5 centimeters
2½ inches	6.25 centimeters
4 inches	10 centimeters
5 inches	12.75 centimeters
6 inches	15.25 centimeters
12 inches (1 foot)	30.5 centimeters

CREDITS

The author and publisher gratefully acknowledge the permission granted to reproduce the copyright material in this book. Every effort has been made to trace copyright holders and to obtain their permission for the use of copyright material. The author and publisher apologize for any errors or omissions in the below list and would be grateful if notified of any corrections that should be incorporated in future reprints or editions of this book.

Page 9 *Smoky Mountain Memories*
Words and Music by Dolly Parton
Copyright © 1994 Velvet Apple Music
All Rights Reserved Used by Permission
Reprinted by Permission of Hal Leonard LLC

Page 21 *Rocky Top*
Words and Music by Felice and Boudleaux Bryant
Reprinted with Permission.

Page 35 *Tennessee River*
Words and Music by Randy Owen
Copyright © 1980 Concord Music Publishing
All Rights Administered by The Bicycle Music Company
All Rights Reserved Used by Permission
Reprinted by Permission of Hal Leonard LLC

Page 41 *Mountain Dew*
Words and Music by Scott Wiseman and Bascom Lunsford
Copyright © 1935, 1945 Sony/ATV Music Publishing LLC and
Three Wise Boys Music, LLC
Copyright Renewed
All Rights on behalf of Sony/ATV Music Publishing LLC
    Administered by Sony/ATV Music Publishing LLC,
    424 Church Street, Suite 1200, Nashville, TN 37219
International Copyright Secured All Rights Reserved
Reprinted by Permission of Hal Leonard LLC

Page 51 *My Tennessee Mountain Home*
Words and Music by Dolly Parton
Copyright © 1972 (Renewed 2000) Velvet Apple Music
All Rights Reserved Used by Permission
Reprinted by Permission of Hal Leonard LLC

Page 63 *Tennessee Stud*
Words and Music by Jimmy Driftwood
Reprinted with Permission.

Page 75 *Dixie Chicken*
Words and Music by Lowell George & Martin Kibbee
Reprinted with Permission.

Page 93 *Tennessee Jed*
Words by Robert Hunter
Music by Jerry Garcia
Copyright © 1972 ICE NINE PUBLISHING CO., INC.
Copyright Renewed
All Rights Administered by UNIVERSAL MUSIC CORP.
All Rights Reserved Used by Permission
Reprinted by Permission of Hal Leonard LLC

Page 121 *Tennessee Whiskey*
Words and Music by Dean Dillon and Linda Hargrove
Copyright © 1981 UNIVERSAL - SONGS OF POLYGRAM
    INTERNATIONAL, INC. and EMI ALGEE MUSIC CORP.
Exclusive Print Rights for EMI ALGEE MUSIC CORP. Controlled
and Administered by ALFRED MUSIC
All Rights Reserved Used by Permission
Reprinted by Permission of Hal Leonard LLC

Page 121 *Tennessee Whiskey*
Words and Music by LINDA HARGROVE and
DEAN DILLON
© 1981 EMI ALGEE MUSIC CORP and UNIVERSAL SONGS OF
POLYGRAM INTERNATIONAL
Exclusive Print Rights for EMI ALGEE MUSIC CORP Controlled
and Administered by ALFRED MUSIC
All Rights Reserved
Used By Permission of ALFRED MUSIC

PHOTOGRAPHY

All photography by Angie Mosier, except where noted.
Pages viii, 2, 3, 4 (bottom), National Park Service archives.
Page 4 (top), The Newport Plain Talk Newspaper.
Pages 6-7, 8, 11, 12, 13, 14-15, 16, 17, 18-19, 20, 22, 25, 28,
    74, 134, 140-141, 143, 150-51, 152, courtesy of Ole Smoky
    Distillery, LLC.
Page 10, courtesy of Jessi Baker.
Pages 73, 83, 85, 135, Christy Bonifacio, Deloise Photography.

INDEX

SHINING

text copyright © 2019 by *Ole Smoky Distillery, LLC*. Photography © 2019 by Angie Mosier. All rights reserved. Printed in China. No part of this book may be used or reproduced in any manner whatsoever without written permission except in the case of reprints in the context of reviews.

Andrews McMeel Publishing
a division of Andrews McMeel Universal
1130 Walnut Street, Kansas City, Missouri 64106

www.andrewsmcmeel.com

www.olesmoky.com

OLE SMOKY, OLE SMOKY TENNESSEE MOONSHINE, OLE SMOKY WHISKEY, and SHINE RESPONSIBLY are registered trademarks of Ole Smoky Distillery, LLC.

19 20 21 22 23 TEN 10 9 8 7 6 5 4 3 2 1

ISBN: 978-1-4494-9700-2

Library of Congress Control Number: 2018964446

Editor: Jean Z. Lucas
Art Director/Designer: Holly Swayne
Production Manager: Carol Coe
Production Editor: Margaret Daniels

Attention: Schools and Businesses
Andrews McMeel books are available at quantity discounts with bulk purchase for educational, business, or sales promotional use. For information, please e-mail the Andrews McMeel Publishing Special Sales Department: specialsales@amuniversal.com.